## A GUIDE TO *THE TOUGH GUIDE*

Imagine that every single fantasy novel featuring kings, dragons, quests, and magic takes place in the same country. That country is called Fantasyland.

Part "travel guide" for the hapless "fantasy tourist" (or "reader"), part send-up of fantasy literature's clichés, Diana Wynne Jones's *The Tough Guide to Fantasyland* is a must-read for every genre fiction fan as well as aspiring writer.

You will never read a sword-and-sorcery novel—or any other kind of fantasy novel, for that matter—the same way again!

# FIREBIRD
### Where Fantasy Takes Flight™

## Books by DIANA WYNNE JONES

### THE DALEMARK QUARTET

Cart and Cwidder
Drowned Ammet
The Spellcoats
The Crown of Dalemark

### THE CHRESTOMANCI BOOKS

Charmed Life
The Magicians of Caprona
Witch Week
The Lives of Christopher Chant
Conrad's Fate
The Pinhoe Egg

### OTHER BOOKS

Changeover
Witch's Business (U.K. Wilkins' Tooth)
The Ogre Downstairs
Eight Days of Luke
Dogsbody
Power of Three
Who Got Rid of Angus Flint?
The Four Grannies
The Time of the Ghost
The Homeward Bounders
Archer's Goon
Fire and Hemlock
Warlock at the Wheel (short stories)
The Skiver's Guide
The Thirteenth Enchanter
Howl's Moving Castle
A Tale of Time City
Chair Person
Wild Robert
Hidden Turnings (editor)

Castle in the Air
Aunt Maria (U.K. Black Maria)
A Sudden Wild Magic
Yes, Dear (picture book)
Hexwood
Fantasy Stories (editor)
Everard's Ride (short stories)
Stopping for a Spell (short stories)
The Tough Guide to Fantasyland
Minor Arcana (short stories)
Deep Secret
Believing Is Seeing (short stories)
Dark Lord of Derkholm
Puss in Boots (retelling)
Mixed Magics (short stories)
The Year of the Griffin
The Merlin Conspiracy
Unexpected Magics (short stories)
The Game (novella)

## OTHER TOUGH GUIDES

*The Tough Guide to Saturn* (Rings excluded)

*The Tough Guide to Boating on Mars*

*The Tough Guide to Flat Worlds*

*The Tough Guide to Transport in the Multiverse*
(mostly by Telephone Box)

*The Tough Guide to Time Warps* (out last century)

*The Tough Guide to Broomstick Flying* (with Free Gift of pointy hat)

*Kobbé's Tough Guide to Space Opera*

*Gandalf's Tough Guide* (includes instructions on
how to lead Tourists into Dark Places and then leave them stranded)

*The Tough Guide to the End of the World* (coming soon)

*The Tough Guide to Black Holes* (unaccountably missing)

# THE TOUGH GUIDE TO FANTASYLAND

## Revised and Updated Edition

## DIANA WYNNE JONES

An Imprint of Penguin Group (USA) Inc.

FIREBIRD
Published by the Penguin Group
Penguin Group (USA) Inc., 345 Hudson Street, New York, New York 10014, U.S.A.
Penguin Group (Canada), 90 Eglinton Avenue East, Suite 700,
Toronto, Ontario, Canada M4P 2Y3 (a division of Pearson Penguin Canada Inc.)
Penguin Books Ltd, 80 Strand, London WC2R 0RL, England
Penguin Ireland, 25 St Stephen's Green, Dublin 2, Ireland
(a division of Penguin Books Ltd)
Penguin Group (Australia), 250 Camberwell Road, Camberwell, Victoria 3124,
Australia (a division of Pearson Australia Group Pty Ltd)
Penguin Books India Pvt Ltd, 11 Community Centre, Panchsheel Park,
New Delhi - 110 017, India
Penguin Group (NZ), Cnr Airborne and Rosedale Roads, Albany, Auckland, 1310
New Zealand (a division of Pearson New Zealand Ltd)
Penguin Books (South Africa) (Pty) Ltd, 24 Sturdee Avenue,
Rosebank, Johannesburg 2196, South Africa

Registered Offices: Penguin Books Ltd, 80 Strand, London WC2R 0RL, England

First published in the UK by Vista, 1996

First published in the United States by DAW Books, by permission of the Cassell Group,
Wellington House, London UK, 1998

This edition published by Firebird, an imprint of Penguin Group (USA) Inc., 2006

Text copyright © Diana Wynne Jones, 1996, 2006
Map by Tony Sahara

ISBN-13: 978-0-7394-7914-8

Printed in the United States of America

For Hannah M. G. Shapero

With particular thanks also to Chris Bell and Paul Barnett

# HOW TO USE THIS BOOK

***WHAT TO DO FIRST:***

1. Find the MAP. It will be there. No Tour of Fantasyland is complete without one. It will be found in the front part of your brochure, quite near the page that says

    > *For Mom and Dad for having me*
    > *and for Jeannie (or Jack or Debra or Donnie or ... ) for*
    > *putting up with me so supportively*
    > *and for my nine children for not interrupting me*
    > *and for my Publisher for not discouraging me*
    > *and for my Writers' Circle for listening to me*
    > *and for Barbie and Greta and Albert Einstein and Aunty May*

    and so on. Ignore this, even if you are wondering if Albert Einstein is Albert Einstein or in fact the dog.

    This will be followed by a short piece of prose that says

    > *When the night of the wolf waxes strong in the morning,*
    > *the wise man is wary of a false dawn.*
    > > *Ka'a Orto'o,* Gnomic Utterances, *VI ii*

    Ignore this too (or, if really puzzled, look up GNOMIC UTTERANCES in the *Toughpick* section). Find the Map.

2. Examine the Map. It will show most of a continent (and sometimes part of another) with a large number of BAYS, OFFSHORE ISLANDS, an INLAND SEA or so and a sprinkle of TOWNS. There will be scribbly snakes that are probably RIVERS, and names made of CAPITAL LETTERS in curved lines that are not quite upside down. By bending your neck sideways you will be able to see that they say things like "Ca'ea Purt'wydyn" and "Om Ce'falos." These *may* be names of COUNTRIES, but since most of the Map is bare it is hard to tell.

    These empty inland parts will be sporadically peppered

with little molehills, invitingly labelled "Megamort Hills," "Death Mountains," "Hurt Range" and such, with a whole line of molehills near the top called "Great Northern Barrier." Above this will be various warnings of danger. The rest of the Map's space will be sparingly devoted to little tiny feathers called "Wretched Wood" and "Forest of Doom," except for one space that appears to be growing minute hairs. This will be tersely labelled "Marshes."

That is mostly it.

No, wait. If you are lucky, the Map will carry an arrow or compass-heading somewhere in the bit labelled "Outer Ocean" and this will show you which way up to hold it. But you will look in vain for INNS, reststops, or VILLAGES, or even ROADS. No—wait another minute—on closer examination, you will find the empty interior crossed by a few bird tracks. If you peer at these you will see they are (somewhere) labelled "Old Trade Road—Disused" and "Imperial Way—Mostly Long Gone." Some of these routes appear to lead (or have led) to small edifices enticingly titled "Ruin," "Tower of Sorcery," or "Dark Citadel," but there is no scale of miles and no way of telling how long you might take on the way to see these places.

In short, the Map is useless, but you are advised to keep consulting it, because it is the only one you will get. And, be warned. If you take this Tour, you are going to have to visit every single place on this Map, whether it is marked or not. This is a Rule.

3. Find your STARTING POINT. Let us say it is the town of Gna'ash. You will find it down in one corner on the coast, as far away from anywhere as possible.

4. Having found Gna'ash, you must at once set about finding an INN, Tour COMPANIONS, a meal of STEW, a CHAMBER for the night, and then the necessary TAVERN BRAWL. (If you look all these things up in the *Toughpick* section, you will know what you are in for.) The following morning, you must locate the

MARKET and attempt to acquire CLOTHING (which absolutely *must* include a CLOAK), a SADDLE ROLL, WAYBREAD, WATER-BOTTLES, a DAGGER, a SWORD, a HORSE, and a MERCHANT to take you along in his CARAVAN. You *must* resign yourself to being cheated over most prices and you are advised to consult a local MAGICIAN about your Sword.

5. You set off. Now you are on your own. You should turn to the *Toughpick* section of this brochure and select your Tour on a pick-and-mix basis, remembering only that you will have to take in all of it, so that it is no use going straight to CONCLUSION. Management Rules will not allow you to do this until you are on your third brochure. With this proviso, you can take anything in any order you please. The Rules are clearly stated in every case and the OFFICIAL MANAGEMENT TERMS (OMTs) have been thoughtfully included in *italics* and marked **OMT** where necessary. All items in CAPITALS can be found in *Toughpick*.

6. Have a good Tour. Thank you for choosing to go with our MANAGEMENT.


## *WHAT TO DO NEXT:*

Consult *Toughpick*.

# IDENTIFICATION ELEMENTS

In order to make this Tough Guide—and your Tour—a more re-warding experience, Management has devised a range of simple Identification Symbols. You will find these next to most entries. Here are the Symbols and their meanings.

Animal

Battle and/or Fighting

Bird

Building

Clan

Cliché

Entertainment

Evil

Fish

Food

Geography

Good

Health

Industry

Landmark

Lodging

Magic

Money

Music

Nature and/or Landscape

Person

Personal Effects

Religion

Royalty

Tool and/or Weapon

Transportation

# TOUGHPICK

*Ask any question you please of the Gods. They do not have to answer.*

*Ka'a Orto'o,*
**Gnomic Utterances,** *II xvi*

**ADEPT.** One who has taken what amounts to the Post-graduate Course in MAGIC. If a MAGIC USER is given this title, you can be sure she/he is fairly hot stuff. However, the title is neutral and does *not* imply that the Adept is either GOOD or EVIL. Examine carefully each Adept you encounter and be cautious, even if she/he seems friendly. See COLOUR CODING for the best way of telling friends from enemies.

**ALLEYS** are the most frequent type of ROAD in a CITY or TOWN. They are always narrow and dark and squishy, and they frequently dead-end. You will escape along them when pursued and also be AMBUSHED there.

See also REFUSE and SQUALOR.

**ALLIGATORS.** Probably extinct in Fantasyland and now to be found only in a mummified state hanging from the rafters of a WIZARD's workroom. If the Alligator is present, it is a sure sign that the Wizard is friendly.

**ALTARS** are of three types:

1. In TEMPLES. These are for SACRIFICES, so they will be waist-high and long enough to contain the supine body of a VIRGIN. The stone top will have grooves for blood, and the whole will be covered with *dry brown stains of a troubling kind* (OMT) from former Sacrifices.

2. In the open, usually on a hilltop. These are of marble and quite simple but handsome, because they are always devoted to a GOOD deity. The size and shape varies, but the general effect is of unassuming potency.

3. In RUINS. These Altars are underground or inside a *pyramidal structure* (OMT). They will sit on a dais at the further, darker end, and be about the size of a laundry hamper, in stone. Approach these with care. Though they undoubtedly hide or contain SECRETS or QUEST OBJECTS you need, they will be set about with magical booby traps that are still operative even after a thousand years. You need to disarm these first, and then possibly the thin shade of the enraged deity after that.

**AMBUSHES** will be of four kinds, and you will have them all:

1. By BANDITS, of the CARAVAN with which you are travelling. This will happen early on in your Tour. It will have been carefully set up, usually by a SPY masquerading as a CARAVAN GUARD. In some narrow place with high sides (*rocky defile* (OMT)) or where there is thick forest on either side of the route, Bandits will first shoot all the Guards and then come pouring down to overwhelm the Caravan. This is where you will part company with the Caravan since nearly everyone but you will be killed. You will just be left for dead.

2. By LEATHERY-WINGED AVIANS a little later on, at night

in a high place. This will be your first light brush with the forces of EVIL. (You can tell the Avians are Evil because they SMELL.) You will fight them off quite easily, but you may be left with a festering wound.

3. By the forces of Evil, upon a group of people you either care about or were depending on for help. You will come upon the evidence of this Ambush some time after the midpoint of your Tour. It will be in a ravine. Here you will find the corpses of your brutally murdered friends being eaten by scavengers. Your rage and grief will be enormous—the more so as you had hoped that this party had made it through to the CITY/WIZARD/KING for help. You must dig graves and proceed.

4. By you, on the forces of Evil. This will be near the end of the Tour, when at last you will be able to turn the tables on the ENEMY, by lying in wait at the top of cliffs beside a *rocky defile* OMT. With luck, you will have help here both from the GOOD King and from assorted Other PEOPLES, usually DWARFS, who will be experts in the art of rolling boulders down on the soldiers of the DARK LORD as they pass below. You, with your now considerable experience of Ambushes, will then attack and finish them off. This will be one of your first victories against the forces of Evil. You will throw up afterwards, but basically you will feel good.

**AMULETS.** One of the many magical protective items to be found throughout Fantasyland. This kind is usually small, made of metal, amber or semi-precious stone, and adapted for hanging round the neck. You may be given yours; you may pick it up among other TREASURE; or you may be forced to obtain one from a MAGIC USER. On many Tours, an Amulet is essential and you must acquire one before going on to the next part. Where not essential, Amulets are still useful, since they can give warning of danger (usually by growing very hot) and, if specially powerful, can either invoke the aid of a God or WIZARD or render the owner invisible.

See also INSCRIPTION, INVISIBILITY, QUEST, and TALISMAN.

**ANCIENT ENGINEERING PROJECTS** tend to litter the landscape in some parts of the continent. Most of them are quite mysterious, and all of them are made of some substance not known to the present inhabitants, often of a greenish colour, or a matte black, though white is not unknown. They will be gigantic. Most of them will be pillars that touch the clouds, but ROADS and broken BRIDGES are common too. It is unknown quite what challenge caused earlier peoples to make things that were so very large. Most of them are no use to anyone.

See also RUINS.

**ANGLO-SAXON COSSACKS** live in the STEPPES and breed HORSES. They try to look like Horses themselves by wearing their hair in ponytails. They ride often, expertly and acrobatically. In fact, they show off rather. Regardless of the fact that winds continually sweep the Steppes, they wear little but sleeveless VESTS and scanty TROUSERS. These people are tough. But, despite riding since early infancy, not one Anglo-Saxon Cossack ever has bandy thighs. Something in their genes prevents this. They are organized normally in CLANS under a supreme chieftain but do not seem to fight among themselves. Nor do they fight other PEOPLES much. Everyone knows better than to mess with them. If called on to fight for GOOD, they muster eventually, but it takes time. Then they are formidable cavalry. Oddly, since their way of life is nomadic, they live in stone fastnesses and rarely use TENTS. On most Tours they are a dreadfully masculine society. Their women wear long SKIRTS and are trained to be wimps.

**ANIMALS.** See ENEMY SPIES, FOOD, and TRANSPORT. Apart from creatures expressly designed for one of these three purposes (and this includes HARES and RABBITS), there appear to be almost no animals in Fantasyland. Any other animal you meet will be the result either of a WIZARD's BREEDING PROGRAMME or of SHAPESHIFTING. You may on the other hand *hear* things, such as roaring, trampling, and frequently the hooting of owls, but these are strongly suspected to be sound effects only, laid on by the Management when it feels the need for a little local colour.

See also DOMESTIC ANIMALS and ECOLOGY.

**ANIMAL SKINS** are much in use and are of four kinds:

1. Trappers' furs. These are occasionally brought south in bundles. As there appear to be no ANIMALS to be trapped, it is likely that these skins are either cunning man-made imitations or imported from another world.
2. Furs worn by NORTHERN BARBARIANS. It is possible that these are also false or imported. Another possibility is that the animals providing these furs are now extinct (see ECOLOGY) and that the famous fur loincloths are handed down from father to son.
3. Leather for BOOTS, VESTS, etc. is again of mysterious origin. (See DOMESTIC ANIMALS.) There are not enough cows to go round, but the leather has to come from *somewhere*.
4. Skins of which the TENTS of DESERT NOMADS are made. Here the source is obvious. Nomads breed HORSES: the

Tents have to be made of horsehide. In fact, it is entirely probable that Horses provide all four kinds of Animal Skin.

**APELIKE CANNIBALS** are small, weak, white, and horrible, but where they exist they occur in great numbers, all bundled together like maggots. They have small clawed hands and small sharp fangs, and it is by sheer numbers and persistence that they overwhelm the unwary Tourist, whom they will then eat raw. They live underground, but not very far underground, often in places like deserted farmhouses where travellers would not expect attack; though they seem to fear daylight, they will come out at dusk as soon as those in the farmhouse have relaxed. Just occasionally they will attack a CAMP or a strayed Tourist in open country. They have the look of degenerate humans. Possibly they have strayed into Fantasyland via H. G. Wells's Time Machine.

**APOSTROPHES.** Few NAMES in Fantasyland are considered complete unless they are interrupted by an apostrophe somewhere in the middle (as in Gna'ash). The only names usually exempt from apostrophes, apart from those of most WIZARDS, heroes, and COMPANIONS on the Tour, are those of some COUNTRIES. No one knows the reasons for this. Nor does anyone really know how an apostrophe should be pronounced, though there are theories:
1. You ignore the apostrophe and simply pronounce the word. (Here Gna'ash=Gnash.)
2. You leave a gap or lacuna where the apostrophe occurs. (Here Gna'ash=Gna-ash.)
3. You make a kind of clucking-sound to stand for the apostrophe. (Here Gna'ash=gna*glunk*ash.) Persons with insecurely mounted tonsils should adhere to one of the other two theories.

**APPRENTICES** are people who are training for a trade or skill, which means they are usually quite young and bad at what they do. Most of the time they are like nurses during an operation, being there only to hand the master his tools. They seem to have to do this for a good many years before they get to do anything more interesting, and it is therefore not surprising that some of them get restless and either try to do the interesting stuff themselves or simply run away and join the Tour. The Rules state that if an Apprentice tries to do the interesting stuff on her/his own it will blow up in her/his face. If she/he runs away, she/he will learn all sorts of things very quickly and also probably prove to be the MISSING HEIR to a Kingdom. Surprisingly, very few Apprentices do run away. If you have one on your Tour, you are in for an eventful time.

**ARISTOCRATIC FEUDALISTS.** There are several branches of this PEOPLE:

1. BAD. Here the COUNTRY is organized into peasants and lords and usually ruled by a bad KING or REGENT. The peasants will live in HOVELS and do all the work. The lords will have all the MONEY and oppress the peasants by taxing, beating, and imprisoning them, and exercising unlimited *droit du seigneur*. The lords will live in CASTLES or MANSIONS, but will spend much of their time at Court, wearing sumptuous clothes and jockeying corruptly for the King's favour. Court will be very elaborate. And everything will be worse if the country is ruled by a bad QUEEN. Usually the arrival of the Tour is the signal for the peasants to revolt.
2. GOOD. This country has the same setup, except that a good King rules it. The lords are therefore honest, polite, and kind to their underlings, and the underlings are prosperous and jolly and do not mind pulling their

forelocks to the gentry. They will turn out in great numbers if the Country goes to WAR, and fight valiantly.

3. Indifferent. This has the same setup, but the King is a nonentity, or is lost, or has failed in his duties. The peasants here will be poor because of crop failure and the lords poor because the peasants are. Generally the Management has little interest in this country. The Tour will pass through very quickly unless one of its number happens to be the MISSING HEIR or a poverty-stricken lord from this place. In the latter case, the Tour will visit his brokendown MANSION.

In all three types, the Tourist should, if possible, go straight to Court. That is always where the interest lies.

**ARMAGEDDON** is the battle that ends the world, usually very fierce and involving both the forces of Good and the legions of the Dark and also anyone else who is able to carry a spear. Armageddons happen quite frequently in Fantasyland, normally at a site specified by PROPHECY early in your Tour. Quite often the Prophecy will pick out one or more of the Tour members in veiled terms (as in "The Sword Bearer" or "She who walks with the gods") and she/he will have to be present before the latest Armageddon can begin. The remarkable thing is that there is still some of Fantasyland left to have the battle in.

**ARMOUR** is, in the opinion of the Management, cheating. This is why it is allowed only to the ARMIES of bad KINGS and MINIONS OF THE DARK LORD, as well as the DARK LORD himself. Warriors of the Dark always wear plate Armour, coloured black, though whether the colour is painted on, stove-blacked on, or intrinsic to the metal is not known. No Tourist should attempt to acquire or wear Armour, unless it is sanctioned by being of special metal, found in a PALACE treasury or DWARVEN FASTNESS, and needed urgently for some special purpose. This Armour will be chainmail of incredible lightness, and it will always be, by lucky chance, an exact fit.

**ARMY.** There are strict Rules about this. Only bad KINGS and the DARK LORD are allowed to raise an Army at the start of a Tour. This will always be vast in numbers. It will trample over everything and devastate the country as it marches, and will get bigger and worse as the Tour goes on. This Army will also use MAGIC in unfair ways. The GOOD are allowed to raise a proper Army to combat the bad one only when it is almost too late, right at the end of the Tour, and the Good Army will somehow avoid either trampling crops or eating off the countryside–probably because the Army of the Dark Lord has eaten it all already. Neither Army will have prostitutes and other camp followers: these are reserved for MERCENARIES only. The Rules also state that the two Armies are very evenly matched, although the Good Army is only about half the size of the other one. Do not worry, however, if you find your side apparently defeated. Your Army may be killed to a man, but Good will triumph all the same.

**ASPECT.** The Aspect of a GODDESS or GOD is the deity manifesting itself through a human by making her/him take on an often shadowy form representing that deity. This can be an ANIMAL or other shape, or sometimes just a kind of light. Deities tend to do this when they want to speed up the action a bit. It is often quite hard on the human and a great shock to any onlookers.

**ASSASSINS, GUILD OF.** The second most frequent guild

after the THIEVES' GUILD. Indeed, it is possible that these are the *only* two, and that in Fantasyland crime is the sole organized activity. Be that as it may, the Assassins are numerous and widespread. They are said to be very good at their job, which is of course killing people for money, and to proceed on all occasions with strict regard to law and protocol. Each member will have trained for years in rather a large number of ways of murdering humans (it is not known whether they also accept commissions to rub out ELVES, GIANTS, etc.) and will be distinguishable by a uniform (often black) or a badge. From one-third of the way through your Tour onwards, you may expect someone to have paid an Assassin to slaughter you. The traditional venue of this murder is a townhouse (Assassins, for some reason, do not operate in open country) or WHARF, so be on your guard in these places. But do not lose sleep over it. As the Assassin approaches you will get *a sense of wrongness* **OMT** or *feeling of being watched* **OMT**, and this should alert you in time. Once alert, you will find it surprisingly easy to kill this practised killer. He will die protesting that you broke some Rule or other.

**ASTROLOGY.** Fantasyland has *strange constellations* **OMT** which MAGES and astrologers frequently consult, often with the help of an instrument called an *astrolabe* **OMT**, which in our world is a primitive sextant but in Fantasyland is probably a zodiacal ready-reckoner. However, the Management is very reticent about the constellations that compose their ZODIAC and about what each of them means, either alone or in conjunction. Consequently a Mage or an astrologer can tell you just what she/he feels like. Usually the Management pays these people to tell you in obscure terms what the STARS say is going to happen in the way of WARS and CATACLYSMS on the Tour, and therefore any prediction they make is bound to come true, provided you can understand it.

See also PROPHECY.

**AVERAGE FOLK** are any people inhabiting the continent who are not specifically mentioned in the list of PEOPLES.

They are not precisely normal all the same. Those who are not ASSASSINS, BEGGARS, or THIEVES will be INNKEEPERS, MERCHANTS, or peasants, and therefore they are busy trying to either rob you, rub you out, or cheat you. The rest will be fully occupied being taxed out of existence or dealing with a variety of magical nuisances. Otherwise they are rather like you, give or take a few hideous sores, gnarled hands, and suspicious scowls. Do not expect help or sympathy from any of them.

**AXE.** The only allowable cutting WEAPON apart from a SWORD. To be allowed one you must be a NORTHERN BAR-

BARIAN, a DWARF, or a BLACKSMITH; most Tourists have to make do with a Sword. WOODSMEN, of course, have Axes too, but not as Weapons.

# B

*Beware, when the landscape is of surpassing beauty, of the needle in the haystack.*

Ka'a Orto'o,
Gnomic Utterances, *XXI vi*

**BACKLASH OF MAGIC** is when a SPELL is either foiled or bungled and the MAGIC recoils. This usually ends up in the face of the one who cast the Spell, often fatally; but occasionally, particularly if the Spell was very large, the Backlash goes on to spray everyone in the vicinity or even travel in waves across the continent. This can be very dangerous. The Rules state that there is no way of stopping Backlash.

**BACKPACKS** are fairly unobtainable, since they do not form part of the regulation equipment for Tourists. The Rule is that the correct form of luggage is a SADDLE ROLL or Saddlebag. When, however, you have got through all available supplies of HORSES, you will find yourself forced to manufacture a Backpack from BLANKETS and harness. Expect to have to do this anytime from halfway to two-thirds of the way through your Tour. This makeshift luggage will prove quite trouble-free. It will not fall to pieces and drop your lunch the way it would if you did the same thing in your own world. It should last you easily to the end of the Tour.

**BALES.** Merchandise of any description (although the Management seldom describes it) is always in Bales, presumably waterproof since you will mostly see Bales on a WHARF. Crates are almost never used. This is peculiar, as timber seems readily available, more so than waterproof fabrics. (See BUILDINGS and CLOAKS.) We put this down to custom or Rules. Bales on Wharfs are always being unloaded by very noisy dockworkers of all sexes.

See also WINE.

**BANDITS** roam the hillier parts of the country in large gangs that seem fairly well organized. They are easily able to plant a SPY or a false GUARD in any CARAVAN (see also CARAVAN GUARD) to lead it into a prepared AMBUSH. Expect to be attacked by Bandits early in the Tour. They will leave you for dead, possibly taking one of your COMPANIONS prisoner before they do. In this case you must prepare to rescue her/ him from the clearing where the Bandits are preparing for a mass rape. You need have no compunction about killing as many Bandits as you can. Male or female, they are the dregs. Nor will they seem very organized when you burst into the clearing. You may steal their HORSES and proceed with the Tour.

Two questions about Bandits remain unanswered. These are:

1. Where are Bandits recruited from? The Management is vague on this point, but sometimes indicates that Bandits are outcasts, on the run for crimes committed in their hometowns or villages, or that they are unattached MERCENARIES.

# HOW TO COMPOSE A BALLAD

You need to start with some lines of well-known Wisdom, like this:

*Why number the teeth of a stallion*
*    you have just received for free,*
*Or swiftly assess and inspect with care*
*    the gulf you must jump for me?*
*Know that an avian held in the fist*
*    weighs more than the flock you see,*
*And among a great surplus of chefs,*
*    your soup might burnèd be.*

Next, include a LEGEND (which turns out to be History and quite accurate), so:

*There once was a monarch, his name was Cole,*
*    who drank and laughed his glee,*
*For beside his throne on seats of stone*
*    sat his lovely daughters three.*
*One was as fair as the dawn's bright air,*
*    the second dark to see,*
*And the third was lovelier still, my lads,*
*    and a wicked one was she.*

After this you will need a chorus, which seems to be nonsense but turns out to be Hugely Significant, like this:

*And they fiddled and they twiddled*
*And they twiddled and they fiddled*
*And they fiddled all night all three.*

Do this two or three more times and you will have your Ballad.

2. What do the Bandits do with the large amount of loot they regularly cull from Caravans? The Management is vaguer still on this point and has never so far indicated the whereabouts of any receivers of stolen goods willing to deal with Bandits, but since the Bandits cannot eat JEWELLERY or baled cloth, such outlets must exist.

Both these questions may have the same answer. The Bandits are employed by the Management to make the early stages of the Tour more interesting.

**BARBARIAN HORDE.** This will be lots and lots of wild-seeming people advancing under a cloud of dust in order to devastate more civilized parts. They are a bit like locusts, except that they kill people direct. Tourists should take cover at once when the telltale dust cloud is sighted, but should not otherwise be too concerned. These Barbarians never harm Tourists and are, in fact, mostly innocent victims. They have usually been stirred up by some God or the DARK LORD. They will often go home quietly when talked to seriously.

See also NORTHERN BARBARIANS.

**BARBARY VIKINGS** wear horned HELMETS and fur CLOAKS; otherwise you could mistake them for NORTHERN BARBARIANS. They swagger hugely, quarrel hugely, drink hugely, and boast hugely. The thing they like best is killing people, particularly lots at once. If a Barbary Viking goes berserk, he will kill even more freely. Stand clear if one does.

All of them are excellent seamen. Their BOATS have square sails and lines of SHIELDS down the sides. Quite often, the Management employs them as PIRATES because they are good at raping and looting and burning, but on some Tours they appear as allies of a rather wilful kind, and will even take Tourists for a sail. At home, which is somewhere quite northerly, they have a KING, who is GOOD and to whom they are violently loyal, and their womenfolk, whom you scarcely see at all because they are all at home breeding warriors. Barbary Vikings are even maler than ANGLO-SAXON COS-SACKS.

**BARDS** are best thought of as musical MAGIC USERS. On former Tours they tended to be diffident people, forced to roam the continent in ragged finery, scraping a poor living by playing and singing in INNS and FAIRGROUNDS. They were not always honest. When their MUSIC proved to have enormous power, they were naively astonished and usually blamed their HARPS. Nowadays the Management is alerted to the powers of Bards and has taken to collecting bardic youngsters into halls or troupes under a master, for stringent professional training. Bards are now required to dress smartly, to play the Harp and at least two other instruments, to have on tap (and sing to professional standards) all available songs and invocations, to memorize all LEGENDS, BALLADS and *old lore* **OMT**, to recite epics and to know a fair number of SPELLS. Thus they frequently join Tours as a powerful COMPANION. You can ask your Bard to open PORTALS and assuage DEMONS and do almost anything musical. She/he will often dredge from memory vital pieces of KNOWL-EDGE that even your Tour MENTOR has missed. Bards are so potent that it is possible they all go on in old age to become MYSTICAL MASTERS. After all, Mystical Masters had to begin somewhere.

**BARONS** occur among most of the ARISTOCRATIC FEU-DALIST Peoples. They are a kind of lord who is not a good thing. Most of them live in huge old (*mouldering* **OMT**) Halls or CASTLES, from which they oppress the peasantry, attack and imprison Tourists, and have dealings with either DEMONS or the less pleasant MAGIC USERS. They have great numbers of ancestors, and their residences are likely to be full of the GHOSTS of these forebears, most of whom were as unpleasant as the present Baron and all of whom met with bad ends. GOOD Barons are almost unknown. If they are Good, they will have another title to add to the "Baron."

**BAR SERVICE** has not yet been invented. Drinks and other orders are traditionally brought to you at your table in the INN by barmaids. This is an enlightened arrangement by the Management because it prevents unemployment among young unmarried women and probably also keeps up the birthrate.

See also EUNUCHS, MAIDS, and WAR.

**BATH** is something all Tourists crave for quite soon. After very few days of slogging along in all weathers and sleeping in your clothes, you will be ready to kill for a Bath. You will crave to wash your hair. The Management is reasonable on this issue. Before long, you will find either a deep POOL in a RIVER of icy water (*icemelt*OMT; see also HYPOTHERMIA, COMMON COLD, and CHILBLAINS) or an INN with a heated bathhouse. You will be able to leave your clothes, money, weapons, and SECRETS on the bank or bathhouse bench and wash in perfect safety. Management Rules state that no one ever steals your clothes/valuables or AMBUSHES you while you are immersed in a Bath. Any lurker will wait until you have finished. Take care, however. Baths are the occasion for SEX with one or more of your FELLOW TRAVELLERS. No matter how irritating you have found her/him up to then, after or during the Bath you will find her/him irresistible. It is probably something in the WATER.

**BAYS** nibble the coastline all over and have three uses:

1. For having fishing VILLAGES where you might hire a small BOAT, provided the villagers are not all out sailing against the sunset.

2. For being washed up in after a shipwreck. This kind of Bay is always a long way from anywhere, rather sandy, and without fresh WATER. Never mind. If you are washed up here, it will be because some vital QUEST OBJECT or Information (see KNOWLEDGE) is waiting nearby in a CAVE for you to discover.

3. For going down to in order to meet SCALY FOLK. This Bay will be rocky and picturesque, the more so because you will probably have to wait for either Moonrise or dawn before the Scaly Folk condescend to emerge from the sea. Be patient. They too have vital Information.

**BED.** This is something all Tourists will soon miss acutely. And when, after days of sleeping outside on the ground, you finally arrive somewhere where there are beds, prepare yourself for disappointment. Beds in Fantasyland are always made of rope wrapped around a frame, with a mattress of straw on top. You will spend the night oozing between the holes among the ropes. And being prickled.

**BEER** always foams and is invariably delivered in tankards. The Management is not concerned with the taste of it. That is your funeral.

**BEGGARS** are to be found in all major CITIES, always wearing rags and often with hideous deformities. They will pester Tourists for money from the City gates onwards. As soon as the City comes under SIEGE, however, all Beggars vanish. The Management has prudently withdrawn them for use in other Cities along the Tourist routes. This makes sense. Beggars would only be in the way during the fighting.

**BEGINNINGS.** Fantasyland, like so many other places, had its Beginnings at a time when no one was around to see it. Nevertheless, quite a lot is known about it. Unlike our world, Fantasyland was definitely made by Gods, working alone or in teams of three, or in whole pantheons. This accounts for some of the peculiarities of the place, since the Rule is that one Goddess or three Gods always made some kind of mistake, often by being distracted somehow during the act of creation; and a pantheon of GODDESSES AND GODS tended to disagree and quarrel, causing mistakes likewise. This, at the very least, let EVIL in. After this, according to the ELVES, the deity/deities took time off to make the Elves and then let a certain amount of evolution happen. Opinions vary as to when and how humanity arrived, but the majority seem to favour the notion that humans were imported from another planet or universe.

**BETRAYAL** is a word widely used on the Tour. It can mean:

1. One of your COMPANIONS lets you down. You can tell by their COLOUR CODING who this is going to be.
2. An ENEMY SPY tells the BANDITS or the MINIONS OF THE DARK LORD where you are. Which is what you would expect.
3. An employee of the DARK LORD shows the ENEMY how to get into the CITY.
4. A COURTIER or rival PRINCE frames the heir to the crown and causes him to be exiled for crimes he did not commit.

   Expect all of these things in the course of the Tour, whatever you think Betrayal means.

**BETS** are laid by soldiers on dice, by everyone on GLADI-ATORS, and by WARRIOR WOMEN on almost anything. Management Rules state that no Tourist will lay a Bet unless he is the SMALL MAN. No Tours so far have been founded on the outcome of a Bet, and only in rare cases are they started by one.

See also GAMING.

**BIRDS.** There are remarkably few Birds in Fantasyland, either in WOODS or on moorland. The reason is probably that, when any Bird is seen, it is promptly shot by a Tourist desperate for something else to eat besides STEW. Otherwise Birds are of three main kinds:

1. The occasional carrier pigeon, for use when no MAGIC USERS are around to exercise MINDSPEECH.

2. Trained hawks/eagles in the employ of EYRIE CLANS. These Birds are larger than their wild cousins (which do not exist), with larger heads. This is because they are telepathic. They have formidable intelligence and acute eyesight, and usually fight to the death beside their owners.

3. ENEMY SPIES, which are nearly always crows. The EN-EMY here exercises remarkably little intelligence. In the virtual absence of all other Birds, the crows are nearly always spotted as SPIES and it rarely seems to occur to any MINION OF THE DARK LORD to disguise these crows as friendly eagles.

See also BREEDING PROGRAMMES, CHICKENS, ENEMY SPIES, and FOOD.

**BIRTHRIGHT.** This is what at least one of the party on the Tour will be looking for and it may indeed turn out to be the main QUEST OBJECT. It is a little on the lines of people from

North America and Australia coming to Europe to find out about their families, but more complicated. There are two kinds of Birthright quested for:

1. Magical. The person in search of Magical Birthright will have inklings of TALENT, but no more. In order to become a proper MAGIC USER she/he will have to seek out a powerful MAGE or WIZARD and try to learn from them. Mere family will not do, unless a parent turns out to be the Wizard, the DARK LORD, or an ENCHANTRESS. And it usually turns out that the Mage/Wizard is no help either. The seeker will have to go through difficult and frightening experiences that make her/him develop her/his Talent out of sheer terror.

2. Family. Here the person seeking Birthright is always a Royal heir. If you are an ordinary person do not expect to discover your family, unless of course you are a MISSING HEIR and had no idea that you were. If you are of Royal birth, then finding out who you are may well happen quite early in the Tour. You will have to spend the rest of it honing your skills as a ruler and collecting lost items of Royal regalia, all of which will proclaim your Birthright. See also ORBS, RINGS, SCEPTRES, and SWORDS.

On some Tours both kinds of Birthright are being sought, occasionally by the same person. This is where it can get complicated.

**BLACK ARTS.** All MAGICS of an unpleasant and antisocial nature. They are often to do with killing and enslaving things and normally require a SACRIFICE as preliminary, or at least a lot of blood. The mark of Black Arts is that the blood is not willingly donated. Practitioners will either trick Tourists and others into donations or seize them and cut them, often with a knife that looks rather unpleasant. There will then be a lot of mumbling and GESTURES around a PENTAGRAM, during which there will be *a sense of wrongness* OMT or *a feeling of extreme cold* OMT; in extreme cases, *terror blooms* OMT. This usually heralds the arrival of a DEMON which is about to get out of control. Practitioners can be of all grades of expertise, from the feeble person who merely wishes for a little power (and gets steadily more corrupted) to the high ADEPT who regularly summons Demons and enslaves ARMIES. Some of them will be adherents of the DARK LORD. Some of them will have set up on their own. Tourists may expect to meet someone who is into the Black Arts at fairly infrequent but regular intervals along the way.

See also NECROMANCY and REEK OF WRONGNESS.

**BLACKSMITHS** are much in evidence, hammering in forges and sometimes even shoeing HORSES. The Rules state that a Blacksmith is huge and brawny but wise and gentle in nature. For this reason Blacksmiths make excellent foster-fathers, either to young Tourists or to MISSING HEIRS. If someone from either of these classes of person needs to reforge a broken SWORD, the Blacksmith can show her/him how. But the Rules also state that two out of three Blacksmiths have a sexy teenage daughter, who will attempt to seduce her foster-brother(s). When this happens, the only course for the fosterling is to leave at once on a QUEST. On his travels, he will soon realize that this young lady is not for him.

**BLANKETS** are to Fantasyland what sleeping bags are to our own world. They are what you will sleep in. Blankets seem very warm. No Tourist ever has more than one. And they seem quite waterproof. It is usually only towards dawn that rain gets through them to the sleeper beneath. All the same, those booked for the Tour must steel themselves for spending many nights shivering. And then the next night, since even in Fantasyland, Blankets do not dry in twelve hours when rolled up behind the saddle.

**BOATS** are always quite small and built of wood. This is to make it easier for them to sink in a STORM, be caught by PIRATES, or overturned by a SEA MONSTER.

The rigging of Boats is puzzling. Small ones seem to be fore-and-aft rigged in a more modern manner than large ones, which always seem to have more of an antique cross-rig. Perhaps this is again so that Pirates can catch them more easily, but it does make problems in contrary winds. Helpful WIZARDS are forced to spend long hours standing either before the mast or in the prow, making wind get into the sails.

See also GALLEYS and SHIPS.

**BOGS** are water-sodden parts of the TERRAIN put there to slow you down when the Forces of the Dark are chasing you. The mud will often be very deep. You could lose HORSES here. You will also nearly lose a COMPANION, who will sink in the mire up to her/his shoulders and have to be pulled out using a makeshift arrangement of rope. After that, you will soon be out of the Bog. Bogs are quite small, unlike the MARSHES, which are another matter.

**BOOTHS** are always there where commerce is going on. They are a cross between a TENT, a SHOP, and a MARKET stall, and are sort of half-permanent. People in them sell everything except FOOD; some of them are barber's stalls—expect to have to bargain even for a haircut. Storytellers have Booths too, and it is here that you will be directed if the Management wishes you to learn a handy LEGEND. It is not known why everyone has Booths instead of something more permanent and rainproof.

**BOOTS.** In Fantasyland these are remarkable in that they seldom or never wear out and are suitable for riding or walking in without the need of SOCKS. Boots never pinch, rub, or get stones in them; nor do nails stick upwards into the feet from the soles. They are customarily mid-calf length or knee-high, slip on and off easily, and never smell of feet. Unfortunately, the formula for making this splendid footwear is a closely guarded secret, possibly derived from nonhumans (see DWARFS, ELVES, and GNOMES).

**BOWS AND ARROWS** are used by ELVES, defenders of a CITY under SIEGE, and WOODSMEN. Tourists are discouraged by the Management from using these WEAPONS, probably because it is so easy to miss with them, whereas anyone can swing a SWORD. Crossbows, being more accurate, are used almost exclusively by bad people.

**BREAD** is quite well known in Fantasyland, but you will seldom get much of it and it will never be fresh. You might be given some to sop up your STEW in an INN of an evening, but in the morning, just as that day's baking should be ready, the Rules state that you will make a hurried departure, having time to grab up only a piece of stale loaf and a hunk of cheese.

**BREEDING PROGRAMMES**—official or unofficial—are quite common, and affect both ANIMALS and people. It is something everyone accepts. Expect to see the results of the following at any time on your Tour:

1. Animals.

   A) By non-MAGIC USERS. ANGLO-SAXON COSSACKS, DESERT NOMADS, EYRIE CLANS, and WOODSMEN all breed either HORSES or BIRDS for greater intelligence, endurance and, in the case of Birds, MINDSPEECH. Their methods are secret, but it is suspected that magical enhancement is often used. The OMT for this is *traditional methods*.

   B) By WIZARDS, who never seem able to refrain from tinkering with genes. Bad Wizards have enormous fun building beasts out of bits and pieces of other creatures, adding wings to bears and lions and snakes and extra legs to birds, and then fangs and slime to the result. The CITADELS of these Wizards are usually surrounded by ill-smelling breeding pits, where all sorts of infant monstrosities are hopping and flopping. GOOD WIZARDS quite often do the same sort of tinkering, but the results are rarely described as monstrous, or as stinking in a breeding pit. Somehow a Good Wizard can cross an eagle, a bear, a lion, and a lizard without the creature being anything but well proportioned, fragrant, and comely. Such beasts are always friendly to humans too (see ECOLOGY). This explains why there are so few large beasts of a normal type in Fantasyland. They have all been captured long ago and interbred with other species.

2. People.

   A) By Royal Families, who are of course mainly concerned that their son/daughter marry only someone else who is Royal. Royalness seems to be a gene, but one which is recessive and easily overwhelmed by common genes. For this reason Royal marriages are always arranged ones. Most of the spirited PRINCESSES joining your Tour will be doing so because a Royal marriage has been arranged for them against their wishes. But there are a few Royal Families where other genes are being preserved and strengthened by judicious marriage. These traits will usually have to do with hereditary ability to speak to GODDESSES AND GODS, hold the SWORD of the Kingdom, or perform major state MAGICS. Ironically, these traits often manifest in long-lost offspring whose descent is far from pure (see MISSING HEIRS).

B) By families of MAGIC USERS intent on preserving or enhancing the family TALENTS. For some reason this is rarely done by coercion or arranged marriage. Someone of the opposite sex and the correct Talent always comes along at the right moment.

c) By WIZARDS again. Bad Wizards tinker with humans and Other PEOPLES to breed them with several more arms and legs or unwholesome dispositions, or both. Sometimes they do this to make convenient SLAVES, sometimes to make better bodies for themselves. Good Wizards will have done this too, but always in the far past. Whole races claim to owe their existence to the Breeding Programme of a long-dead Good Wizard.

**BRIDGES.** The inhabitants of Fantasyland seem to have a distrust of Bridges, maybe because they provide an easy way for an invading ARMY to cross to a VILLAGE on the other side of the RIVER. This is a great inconvenience to the Tourist. The Rule is that, when being pursued by the forces of the Dark, you are going to need to cross a Bridge, and there will be no Bridge. While the Tour is waiting to find a way across, the forces of the Dark have time to catch up. Even if there is supposed to be a Bridge on the route, you are likely to arrive to find it broken—whereupon the forces of the Dark gain steadily again. The only Bridges sure to be still in place are ANCIENT ENGINEERING PROJECTS, and they will be huge, with, as soon as you get to the middle, a tendency to develop a small but impassable gap right at the apex.

**BRIGANDS.** See BANDITS.

**BUILDING MATERIALS** bear little relation to what is available locally. Thus all ordinary houses are made of wood and plaster, even if there is no forest for miles, and all major BUILD-INGS are of stone, regardless of the fact that Fantasyland appears to have no quarries. In the case of Wizards' TOWERS, the stone is always of some notable color, such as red, black, or blue. Possibly this is a side effect of the no-entry spells that the Rules state must always be present. Northern-based WIZARDS and ENCHANTRESSES favour ice as a Building Material, and often have fantastic PALACES carved magically out of glaciers.

ANCIENT ENGINEERING PROJECTS are made of another substance entirely. This seems no longer obtainable.

**BUILDINGS.** The Rule is that all ordinary houses are made mostly of timber, with a tendency to lean off the true. Those in CITIES always have the upper storey jutting out over the street so that the occupants can empty chamber pots on passersby. PALACES and TEMPLES are probably made of stone, but this is so ornamented that no Tourist can be sure. The Rule is that the Tour slams to a stop while the Management draws your attention to every pillar and most gargoyles. No interior, except in HOVELS, is ever simple. The Rules further state that all Buildings seem larger inside than out. Passages, stairs, and halls abound, and every Building you enter will have at least one mysterious shut door leading to somewhere that does not fit the ground plan. Windows are glazed and often have diamond panes, making it hard to see the painted decorations on the walls and very difficult to see out at all.

See also BUILDING MATERIALS, CASTLES, CITADELS, and TOWERS.

**C**

*Certain Sages encountered the hero Somplac one day, who challenged them with the words, "Which is mightier—the mind or the sword?" To which the Sage Algeron answered, "What the sword does, the mind has already accomplished." "True," replied Somplac, "but my answer is more cutting." And he sliced off the left big toe of Algeron.*

*Ka'a Orto'o,*
**Gnomic Utterances,** *V xvi*

**CAMPS** are of two kinds:

1. For ARMIES and MERCENARIES. These consist of many orderly rows of TENTS, with the commander's tent in the middle and sentries regularly patrolling the outskirts. There will be provision carts and the cookhouse Tent (making STEW) in one quadrant, and pickets for HORSES in another. The odd thing here is that, when you look down upon the ENEMY camp from a convenient hillside, you will be able to tell the size of the Army not by counting Tents but by the numbers of cooking fires you see. When you enter the Camp, cooking fires are not in evidence unless required to be scattered, setting fire to Tents, thereby causing the numerically hugely superior Enemy to panic.

2. For Tourists. You will have one of these every night, either in the open under a windy rock or in woodland under dripping TREES. Here you will picket and feed Horses, light a fire and cook Stew, and spread your

bedroll and sleep. First, however, you must dig a latrine pit, and the MAGIC USER among you must set WARDS to keep you all safe at night. Tourists often make the mistake of leaving the latrine outside the Wards, and occasionally the Horses too. This means that you could lose a COMPANION and several mounts to MUTANT NASTIES or other marauders in the night. It is often simpler to arrange to be awake in turns. Whichever, you are going to be glad to sleep under any roof before long.

**CAPITAL LETTERS** at the beginnings of words are used liberally by the Management according to Rules that transcend human understanding and may under no circumstances be questioned (see TABOO).

**CARAVAN GUARDS** are men drawn from all PEOPLES, though human is preferred, and set to ride with a MERCHANT's CARAVAN and protect it from BANDITS. They are of four kinds:

1. Unattached MERCENARIES. These are quite nice guys. Some of them even have NAMES. Tourists need not, however, trouble to get to know this class of GUARD. They will all be killed when the Bandits attack.
2. Unattached nobles or PRINCES. You should cultivate these. They will survive the Bandits' attack and then act as your guides for the next phase of your Tour.
3. Bandits in disguise. This is a frequent class of Guard. They will lead you into an AMBUSH and there is nothing you can do to stop them (see also ENEMY SPIES). Tourists should, however, remember that this Ambush always happens early in a Tour and is therefore usually survived. The Tourist will merely be left for dead.
4. Unattached and/or penniless Tourists. You may find you

have to take service as a Guard in order to proceed with your Tour. If you are strong and know how to use a SWORD it helps, but Merchants seldom check on fighting skills. And your service will last only until the Bandits attack and leave you for dead.

**CARAVANS** in Fantasyland are not the colourful conveyances of Gypsies. They are always a cumbrous train of wagons, wains, and HORSES, with CARAVAN GUARDS, and carry merchandise and occasional passengers along prescribed routes for profit. Probably very few make it to their destinations, given the frequency of BANDITS and other marauders. Tourists, however, are always booked into a Caravan. Any other mode of travel is said to be even less safe. It is therefore odd that most Tourists find themselves in much less trouble as soon as the Caravan has been AMBUSHED and they are free to proceed on their own.

**CASTLES** occasionally adorn the heights for pictorial effect, but the Management usually arranges for you to see round only the obligatory Castle at the centre of a TOWN or CITY. These are edifices with *frowning battlements* (OMT), slit windows, and multiple defensible spiral stairways inside. They contain few or no comfortable rooms, but this does not matter. You will be there under SIEGE, along with the last remaining defenders. These will be running out of arrows and preparing boiling oil to pour through holes in battlements and above the portcullis. When things have got to this pass, most Tourists will be able to depart through the cellar by means of a SECRET PASSAGE; the doomed defenders will be remarkably decent—even jolly—about the fact that you are deserting them like this in their hour of need.

**CATACLYSM.** There has always been at least one of these in Fantasyland, usually in the far past; it reduced the country to a primitive state. But stay alert. A Cataclysm during the present Tour is not to be ruled out, particularly if one of your COMPANIONS annoys or challenges a WIZARD.

**CAVERNS** are large underground systems with RIVERS running through them. They can be entered from SECRET PASSAGES, behind WATERFALLS, and from holes in the hillside. At first there will be large grottoes with stalactites, followed, when your torch fails, by areas that glow on their own. Shortly you will come upon a major centre of population, which can be of Other PEOPLES or of troglodytic humans. Here you will be prudent to buy a BOAT (or steal one if the Cavern Dwellers are hostile), load yourselves, your wounded, and any provisions aboard it, and set off down the underground River. Your least favourite COMPANION will probably die at this point. After quite a few days you will come out in a Hidden VALLEY, often occupied by DRAGONS. This is the main way in which male Tourists get to meet Dragons and you should not miss the experience. Even if there are no Dragons, all Tourists must expect to spend some days in a Cavern at some point in the Tour.

**CAVES** are smaller systems than CAVERNS and are usually entered from somewhere beside a Blocked MOUNTAIN PASS. You will stumble upon a Cave either under a snowdrift or behind a jut of rock just as night falls and you are too exhausted to continue. There will be a stony front CHAMBER big enough for HORSES and a cooking fire for STEW, and a further Chamber at the back which you will not discover straightaway. When you do, you will find it contains either the missing ORB or SCEPTRE you wanted or a carefully wrapped pile of parchment SCROLLS which will give you the KNOWLEDGE you needed. The Management has directed you to this Cave on purpose.

**CHAMBER** is the regular word for your room at an INN and for rooms in any other old buildings. This may be to distinguish them from ordinary houses (*the room at the back of the hovel appeared to be a sleeping place* OMT) or PALACES. But even here the throne room can be a Chamber, as in *silence fell throughout the whole vast Chamber* OMT. CAVES have Chambers too, if you are proposing to sleep in them, and TORTURE is generally done in a specially designated Chamber. Perhaps the Management just likes the word.

**CHICKENS** are seen only after they have been cooked and then only in PALACES, where the Rule is that you eat chicken drumsticks with your fingers and then throw the bones to the dogs. Eggs are very rare. The hens of Fantasyland do not seem to lay very well. They seem to be bred in unseen Palace poultry yards purely for the pot.

**CHILBLAINS** are unheard of, however inclement the WEATHER. This is probably because the Management lives mostly in California.

**CHILDREN** are not commonly found on a Tour. If a Child appears and seems to wish to take part, be very wary. She/he is likely to be either a God or the MISSING HEIR to a Kingdom. In either case this will make the Child unpredictable and capricious. She/he will unquestionably involve you in a great deal of trouble.

See THIEVES' GUILD for the only exception to this Rule.

**CITADELS** are very strong BUILDINGS of thick black stone made for defence. They are tall, with few and slitty windows. Spiral staircases lead to a battlemented top with a very wide view. Most Citadels are at the centre point of a CITY and are where you will all retreat when the ENEMY has got inside the City walls and is burning and sacking there. Naturally you will not need to surrender. Down inside the Citadel are SECRET PASSAGES *carved from the living rock*(OMT) through which you can escape into a CAVERN. Usually you will have to leave quite a few defenders behind. Just occasionally, the Citadel will belong to an Evil WIZARD. In this case it will be all alone, perched on a black crag that proves to be *honeycombed with passages*(OMT), and the Tour will get in through these.

See also CASTLES and CONFRONTATIONS.

**CITIES** occur at the rate of one, or at the most two, to every COUNTRY. They are usually where the ruler lives, and they are surrounded by high stone walls. For these reasons, they are going to be under SIEGE around the time the Tour arrives in them. Prepare for HARDSHIP as soon as you see the walls in the distance. But first prepare for a lot of noise and people (see BEGGARS) and horsedrawn traffic. There will also be multiple ALLEYS (where all the HORSE droppings get pitched), many squares, and some fine houses. The CASTLE or PALACE of the ruler will be on a hill in the exact centre, with TEMPLES somewhere near. The heads of malefactors or enemies of the state will be on stakes somewhere—you may recognise one of them as having belonged to a GOOD man you encountered earlier and rather liked—or perhaps there will be picked-clean skeletons hanging in cages along the sides of the streets, performing the same function as streetlamps, except after dark (see also EXECUTIONS). It is usually quite easy to get into a City through the gates in the walls, but not so easy to get out. When you wish to get away, you will find the gates are shut at sunset and are guarded at all times; you will need to bluff your way through or adopt a disguise. But this does not apply to Siege. The Rule is that, in a Siege situation, you will be glad to stay there and help until eventually you escape, leaving the plucky citizens to their fate.

See also CITY OF CANALS, CITY OF WIZARDS, OLD RUINED CITY, and WALLED CITY.

**CITY OF CANALS**. This CITY is usually on a south or south-facing coast and under the governance of MERCHANT FEUDALISTS at their most crooked. The City is pretty old and seems to have grown up from settlements on a great number of islands in a large RIVER delta; after a while, the channels between island and island have become the canals (*dark* OMT, *scummy* OMT) and on their banks houses have been built upon houses, mostly of timber (*rotting* OMT), with WHARFS on top of that and BRIDGES on and around those. The result is a labyrinth of watery ways known only to the inhabitants, who mostly get about in old, cranky BOATS. The ruling MERCHANTS always live somewhere at the centre in very beautiful houses built of imported stone. They are totally ruthless about wringing their money's worth out of the poorer folk and everything else, and their laws are draconian. Not surprisingly, the THIEVES' GUILD is very strong here; one of the Merchants is probably its Guild-master. Murders are frequent, and bodies drift up and down the canals along with other REFUSE. The whole City smells.

It is essential that Tourists find some kind of native guide in this place, or their throats will be cut before nightfall (see DANGER), but, with any luck, the Management will have thought of this, and one of the Tour COMPANIONS will turn out to have been born here. Failing that, there will be a young lad to help (see THIEVES' GUILD). As a Tourist, you will be here to wring some QUEST OBJECT or SECRET out of the paranoically defended home of the beastliest of the Merchants. You will be so lucky. But then Tourists always are.

**CITY OF WIZARDS** is normally quite a GOOD thing, since only Good WIZARDS seem able to live together. This CITY will be on a hill in someplace that is hidden/hard to get to and surrounded by inviting green lands tilled by non-Wizard underlings, who also perform all domestic chores. Houses will be of stone, often white, and their shapes gracious but odd. Perspective and distances will be a bit strange too. If the effect of all this is rather stately, the City will be full of white-robed MYSTICAL MASTERS, out of whom no one will be able to get any sense. If the effect is more homely, the Wizards will be more like human beings and may quarrel a lot—in fact, they will seldom agree on anything. If the place is organized as a college, do not expect anything but Wizardly bickering.

There have been Cities of EVIL Wizards in the past. Tours will occasionally come across the sites of these, reduced to glassy slag during the ultimate disagreement.

**CLANS.** EYRIE CLANS (obviously), DESERT NOMADS, and OTHER CONTINENTALISTS are always organized in Clans. ANGLO-SAXON COSSACKS and BARBARY VIKINGS sometimes are, and at times most other countries have them one way or another. Clandom is supposed to be a very close and special bonding. Certainly a member of a Clan can call upon all other members in an emergency and they will come flocking in to help. But the easiest way to think of it is as a civilized word for TRIBE, where the obligations are just the same. In the VESTIGIAL EMPIRE, the word for Clans or Tribes is Houses, because the Empire is even *more* civilized. Houses have Politics, where Clans do not. Clans and Houses both give rise to ELITE.

See also POLITICS.

**CLIFF DWELLINGS.** See EYRIE CLANS, though some Other PEOPLES have them too. The average Cliff Dwelling is high up, and approached by a rocky hidden staircase of prodigious length. When you finally gasp your way to the top, you will be instantly challenged by an alert sentry carrying an outsized BIRD. If he is satisfied that your business is important enough, he will then lead you through a hitherto unnoticed gap in the rock. Within, a natural CAVE will have been infinitely enlarged to make rooms, passages, galleries, and storeplaces, most—but not all—with cunningly disguised windows in the cliff face. It will be very chilly (see HEATING), but only you will notice the chill. The place will be organized like a barracks, but the FOOD is always better than the Fantasyland norm. You will get butter, honey, fresh BREAD, and probably not STEW. The Dwellers, though austere, will be friendly and you can take a well-earned rest from DANGER and HARDSHIP here.

**CLOAKS** are the universal outer garb of everyone who is not a Barbarian. It is hard to see why. They are open in front and require you at most times to use one hand to hold them shut. On horseback they leave the shirtsleeved arms and most of the torso exposed to wind and WEATHER. The OMTs for Cloaks well express their difficulties. They are constantly *swirling and dripping* and becoming *heavy with water* in rainy Weather, *entangling with trees* or *swords*, or needing to be *pulled close around her/his shivering body*. This seems to suggest they are less than practical for anyone on an arduous Tour. But they do have one advantage. Female Cloaks usually add a wide frilly hood, male cloaks a wide plain one, and neither of these adjuncts ever gets blown from the head or lets water in round the edges. So at least your head is dry.

It is thought that the real reason for the popularity of Cloaks is that the inhabitants like the look of themselves from the back.

**CLOTHING.** Although this varies from place to place, there are two absolute rules:

1. Apart from ROBES, no garment thicker than a SHIRT ever has sleeves.
2. No one ever wears SOCKS.
   See also CLOAKS, COSTUME, and KNITTING.

**COATS** do not exist in Fantasyland—CLOAKS being universally preferred—but TURNCOATS do.

**COINAGE** has various names, according to which Tour you choose, and will seem to be made of gold, silver, and copper. Adjust to inflation and think of it in dollars: a gold coin = $5, a silver coin = $1, and copper coins are cents. This system is easier than most European currencies.

See also MONEY.

**COLOUR CODING** is very important in Fantasyland. Always pay close attention to the colour of the CLOTHING, hair, and eyes of anyone you meet. It will tell you a great deal. Complexion is also important: in many cases it is coded too.

1. Clothing. Black garments normally mean EVIL, but in rare

cases can mean sobriety, in which case a white ruffled collar will be added to the ensemble. Grey or red clothing means that the person is neutral but tending to Evil in most cases. Any other colour is GOOD, unless too many bright colours are worn at once, in which instance the person will be unreliable. Drab colour means the person will take little part in the action, unless the drab is also torn or disreputable, when the person will be a loveable rogue.

2. Hair. Black hair is Evil, particularly if combined with a corpse-white complexion. Red hair *always* entails magical POWERS, even if these are only latent. Brown hair has to be viewed in combination with eyes, whose colours are the real giveaway (see below), but generally implies niceness. Fair hair, especially if it is silver-blond, *always* means goodness.

3. Eyes. Black eyes are invariably Evil; brown eyes mean boldness and humour, but not necessarily goodness; green eyes *always* entail TALENT, usually for MAGIC but sometimes for MUSIC; hazel eyes are rare and seem generally to imply niceness; grey eyes mean POWER or healing abilities (see HEALERS) and will be reassuring unless they look silver (silver-eyed people are likely to enchant or hypnotise you for their own ends, although they are not always Evil); white eyes, usually blind ones, are for wisdom (never ignore anything a white-eyed person says); blue eyes are always GOOD, the bluer the more Good present; and then there are violet eyes and golden eyes. People with violet eyes are often of Royal birth and, if not, *always* live uncomfortably interesting lives. People with golden eyes just live uncomfortably interesting lives, and most of them are rather fey into the bargain. Both these types should be avoided by

anyone who only wants a quiet life. Luckily, it seldom occurs to those with undesirable eye colours to disguise them by ILLUSION, and they can generally be detected very readily. Red eyes can *never* be disguised. They are EVIL and surprisingly common.

4. Complexion. Corpse-white is Evil, and it grades from there. Pink-faced folk are usually midway and pathetic. The best face-colour is brown, preferably tanned, but it can be inborn. Other colours such as black, blue, mauve, and yellow barely exist.

So, if your acquaintance is wearing green and is blue-eyed and brown-faced, she/he will be OK. *Caution*: Do not apply these standards to our own world. You are very likely to be disappointed.

**COMBAT RING.** See PRACTICE RING and SCHOOL OF WEAPONRY.

**COMMON COLD.** This is one of many viral nuisances not present. You can get as wet, cold, and tired as you like, and you will still not catch cold. But see PLAGUE.

**COMMON TONGUE.** See LANGUAGES.

**COMPANIONS** are chosen for you by the Management. You will normally meet them for the first time at the outset of the Tour. They are picked from among the following: BARD, FE-MALE MERCENARY, GAY MAGE, IMPERIOUS FEMALE, LARGE MAN, SERIOUS SOLDIER, SLENDER YOUTH, SMALL MAN, TALENTED GIRL, TEENAGE BOY, UNPLEASANT STRANGER, and WISE OLD STRANGER. Most parties will have at least one of these and may also occasionally include one or two of the other PEOPLES, usually small ones.

**CONCLUSION.** For this you will have to undertake the third (or possibly the fifth) Tour of the trilogy. If you do not immediately book for the whole set, you may well find yourself stranded halfway across the continent without having completed your QUEST or discovered your BIRTHRIGHT. And the DARK LORD will still be a menace. A little extra money will soon dispel these inconveniences, and you may then have the pleasure of seeing the continent torn asunder in the Final CONFRONTATION. This is a spectacular sight and should not be missed.

**CONFRONTATIONS.** These will occur with mounting intensity as the Tour proceeds, and will fall into one or other of the following classes:

1. Small Friendly Confrontations. This will be when you meet your Tour COMPANIONS and the MERCHANT in whose CARAVAN you intend to travel. Later, you meet a friend aboard the Slave GALLEY or in contest as a GLADIATOR. You then encounter TRAVELLING FOLK and a SEER or Astrologer (see ASTROLOGY). You have an argument with your SWORD or an ORB. You chat up a SLAVE of the opposite sex. You hire a Necromancer (see NECROMANCY). You receive reports from a GOOD SPY. You encounter an old General of the VESTIGIAL EMPIRE/the WEAPONMASTER. You have solemn meetings with EYRIE CLANS/WOODSMEN and telepathic BIRDS. A HERB-WOMAN/HEDGE WIZARD/HEALER comes to your rescue in the MOUNTAINS. A BARD recites to you a vital LEGEND.

2. Small Hostile Confrontations. This term refers to the intruder with a DAGGER in your CHAMBER in the INN, the AMBUSH by BANDITS, and your first brush with the forces of the Dark. You also spot a SPY. Later there are

PIRATES on the INLAND SEA and a MINION OF THE DARK LORD on the OTHER CONTINENT. You are brought before an ENCHANTRESS. You are almost killed by a hostile COURTIER/beard a fat PRINCE/have to spend time with a BARON. You are caught by a prehensile TREE. You face down GUARDS and torturers. You are captured by GOBLINS and their chieftain insults you. You come up against WERES, who are not open to reason.

3. Small Ambiguous Confrontations. You meet your Tour MENTOR and the UNPLEASANT STRANGER. You are cheated by a FERRYMAN or RIVER Travellers. You have a run-in with DWARFS, GNOMES, or DESERT NOMADS. You try to get MONEY from a COUNCIL. You meet a GHOST/ELEMENTAL. You are captured by MARSH DWELLERS and have LANGUAGE problems. You come upon a NUNNERY and talk to the survivor. You try to persuade ISLANDERS that their ISLAND is about to be inundated. The Tour enters a VILLAGE and is rendered uncomfortable by the attitude of the Dwellers. You make the mistake of looking into a Prophetic POOL.

4. Medium-Sized Friendly Confrontations. You meet your first KING or the VESTIGIAL EMPEROR. Later you talk to a DRAGON or friendly DEMON. You stay the night with a Good WIZARD, who shows you some remarkable pieces of KNOWLEDGE. You find ELVES, a college of WITCHES, enter a CITY, or attempt to understand a MYSTICAL MASTER. You persuade a HIGH PRIESTESS to help you and your COMPANIONS. You arrive at the STEPPES/SNOWBOUND NORTH and run into crowds of ANGLO-SAXON COSSACKS/BARBARY VIKINGS/NORTHERN BARBARIANS. You are told home truths by a STONE CIRCLE.

5. Medium-Sized Hostile Confrontations. You face a HIGH PRIEST and his deity, a REGENT, a bad or puppet KING.

You try to get the better of an Evil COUNCILLOR. You reject the overtures of a bad QUEEN. You face and repulse hostile MAGICS. You fall foul of RELIGION in the FANATIC CALIPHATES. You come face-to-face with an Evil WIZARD or a red-eyed MINION OF THE DARK LORD. You fight a MONSTER or two. You confront the ENEMY in a SIEGE.

6. Medium-Sized Ambiguous Confrontations. You encounter loose lumps of MAGIC or guardians of a QUEST OBJECT or enter the HIDDEN KINGDOM and attempt to make sense of its inhabitants. You try to argue with a WOOD.

7. Large Friendly Confrontations. You and your COMPANIONS tout for support among the GOOD rulers. There is a long and verbose COUNCIL OF WAR.

8. Large Hostile Confrontations. There is all-out WAR between GOOD and EVIL. You face down the strongest of the MINIONS OF THE DARK LORD.

9. The Final Confrontation, or Last Battle. You get your chance to finish the DARK LORD at last. In the process a large part of Fantasyland gets destroyed.

**COOK.** Presiding over all KITCHENS is the Cook, who can be male or female, although males predominate in CASTLES and PALACES and females in INNS. Every single one of them has a filthy temper. This gets worse in direct proportion to the amount of cooking they do, and is clearly even worse if the Cook is required to cook something else besides STEW. Any scullion or Kitchen helper in reach during these trying times is bound to have an awful experience. But there is a bright side. Cooks divide into fat and thin. Fat Cooks are really kindly underneath, in which case the Kitchen helper has extra food to look forward to. Thin Cooks, on the other hand, are mean right through. In this case the Kitchen helper can look forward only to an evening without supper and maybe a beating too.

**COSTUME.** It is a curious fact that, in Fantasyland, the usual Rules for CLOTHING are reversed. Here, the colder the climate, the fewer the garments worn. In the SNOWBOUND NORTH, the BARBARIAN HORDES wear little more than a fur loincloth and copper wristguards (see CHILBLAINS and HYPOTHERMIA). However, as one progresses south to reach the ANGLO-SAXON COSSACKS, one finds VESTS and BOOTS added to this costume. Further south still, the inhabitants of the VESTIGIAL EMPIRE wear short SKIRTS and singlets and add to this a voluminous wrapper on cold days. Thereafter, clothing steadily increases in thickness and quantity, until one finds the DESERT NOMADS in the tropics muffled to the eyebrows in layers of ROBES (see HEATSTROKE).

**COUNCIL.** Although other Councils exist, this term refers primarily to the group of twelve or so unpleasing men who rule the MERCHANT FEUDALISTS, because they do not trust one another enough to let one person do the ruling. The OMT for these is *corrupt*, but they are also cruel and greedy, and they will combine to get rid of anyone who seems to threaten their power. Most Tours do this, so be prepared for Councils to have you Assassinated or put in PRISON on sight. You will find the Council meeting in a lavish *CHAMBER*(OMT) with a breathtakingly ornamental ceiling and gold everywhere. Likely they will be eating and drinking gourmet stuff as well, and each member will have different gorgeous ROBES, covered with JEWELS and gold EMBROIDERY. Some will be piggishly (*swinishly*(OMT)) fat, some thin and wrinkled, but it makes no difference. They are all pure poison. Above all avoid being owed MONEY by them: you will never get it.

**COUNCILLORS** are those who advise a KING. Nine-tenths of them are EVIL. These will be of youngish middle age, with nothing aside from the *REEK OF WRONGNESS* **OMT** to give away the fact that they report directly to the DARK LORD. They will be busy giving the King bad advice and generally messing up the COUNTRY, and they will not welcome the Tour at all. After making efforts to send it on its way, they will normally contrive to have every Tourist imprisoned. You must escape and *unmask* **OMT** the Councillor concerned. The other tenth of Councillors are GOOD and grave and elderly. Many of them have been soldiers. You can rely on them to *understand* **OMT** when the monarch does not.

**COUNTRIES** have ill-defined boundaries, but on the whole correspond to each of the PEOPLES listed, although under various names at the whim of the Management. Most will be ruled by KINGS, TYRANTS, REGENTS, CLAN Chieftains, or members of a priestly caste. The exception is any country of the MERCHANT FEUDALISTS, where the ruling class trusts one another so little that they rule as a COUNCIL. Do not expect democracy anywhere. Do not expect, either, to find one Country bordering on another: there are always large empty/ungoverned areas in between, where there will be forests, WASTE AREAS, or even VILLAGES. No ruler since the VESTIGIAL EMPIRE seems to have got her/his act together sufficiently to claim this spare land.

**COURTIERS** are mainly extras hired by the Management for all scenes in PALACES. Male and female Courtiers will be standing or strutting about, wearing the richest and most exaggerated fashions, and staring or gasping at the manners and dress of the Tourists. Courtiers never sit down. They whisper in groups, trying to gain the favour of the monarch. Very few of them are nice people. If they are, they will be quite young, with NAMES like Daren or Lynthelle, and they will help you a lot with the strange customs at Court. Nasty Courtiers have sneering names like Blyfil and Myrna. If you learn their Names it will be because the man will challenge you to a duel (and possibly POISON his sword tip) and the woman will make bitchy remarks and spread rumours. Myrna often turns out to be a MAGIC USER too. She will cast SPELLS to make all Tourists look fools and to seduce any male Tourists.

**CRONE.** On most Tours a ragged old woman, sometimes of a wild and sinister demeanour, tends to crop up by the way-side in moments of stress, *hobbling* **(OMT)** and *cackling* **(OMT)**. If the Tour has lost its way, she will misdirect it, usually throwing in a few GNOMIC UTTERANCES of a depressing nature as she does so. If the Tour takes in a public EXECU-TION, this Crone will be present at it *busily knitting* **(OMT)**. Since KNITTING is not a normal mortal skill, it is clear that this old lady is an ASPECT of some GODDESS or other.

**CRYSTAL** can be almost any colour. It can be set in a RING, suspended on a chain as a pendant, or be just a lump on its own. It is Fantasyland's equivalent of the telephone, with attached vision. Through Crystal, most MAGIC USERS and some ordinary people can communicate with the WIZARD of their choice over quite long distances. The operator simply leans over the Crystal and concentrates. Shortly a small but extremely clear image of the Wizard forms within it and can be heard to speak. Crystal usually takes over where MINDSPEECH leaves off.

See also CRYSTAL BALL.

**CRYSTAL BALL.** You look into one of these and see

*vapours swirling like clouds*   OMT. These shortly clear away to show a sort of video without sound of something that is going to happen to you soon. It is seldom good news.

See also CRYSTAL and PROPHECY.

**CUPS** are goblets that look rather like golf trophies. You can tell they are important because nobody tries to drink out of them. This is actually silly, because the least a Cup can do is negate POISON. Cups either turn up in hoards of TREASURE or are carefully hidden, packed in a casket, under an ALTAR or somewhere similar. Just occasionally, an ENCHANTRESS will flourish one at you. You will want to take it away from her. This Cup is your QUEST OBJECT. It has Powers, though these are often vague and not always demonstrated. Probably it is best to think of a Cup as a sort of superGrail.

**CURSES** are long-standing ill-wishings which, in Fantasyland, often manifest as semi-sentient. They have to be broken or dispelled. The method varies according to the type and origins of the Curse:

1. Curses on lands. These can be caused either by defects in the KING or lord or by direct malevolence of the DARK LORD. Usually the land turns to Waste in various ways, but if it is a true Curse, there will be a slimy lump of miasma somewhere, or a MONSTER exuding EVIL. You have to find this and torch it.

2. Curses on families. These will have been put on generations ago, causing the family to lose money, to give birth to cripples, and generally to be low and disheartened. These Curses are difficult. The correct way to raise one is to get the person who did it to take it off. But she/he is probably dead by now. Sometimes a descendant can

do as well. If not, the best thing is to force the family into some noble deed on behalf of a God. The God can then remove the Curse.

3. Curses on BUILDINGS. You can tell when a Building (usually a MANSION) is Cursed: it will feel cold as a grave, and some of the roof will be missing and pieces will keep dropping off on you. This type of Curse probably takes a PRIEST or WIZARD and an exorcism to raise. For some reason, DEMONS usually have a hand in this sort of Curse.

4. Curses on RINGS and SWORDS. You have problems. Rings have to be returned whence they came, preferably at over a thousand degrees Centigrade, and the Curse means you won't want to do this. Swords usually resist all attempts to raise their Curses. Your best course is to hide the Sword or give it to someone you dislike.

5. Curses on people. Here the one laying the Curse has obtained your toenail, one of your hairs, or your true NAME, and possibly also made a wax image of you which she/he proceeds to mistreat. You will have racking pains and monstrous bad luck until you find the missing bit of you and get it back.

6. Curses with conditions. These are the easy kind. The Curser has probably stated that the Curse will be lifted only when the INLAND SEA is dry. You just have to arrange for this to happen.

# D

*Doras II was a somewhat absentminded king. It is said that, when Death came to summon him, Doras granted Death the usual formal audience and then dismissed him from his presence. Death was too embarrassed to return until many years later.*

Ka'a Orto'o,
Gnomic Utterances, *LIV iii*

**DAGGERS** are of three main kinds:

1. A slender stabbing WEAPON worn on the belt, in the boot, or up the shirtsleeve as backup to the SWORD, or as the thing with which your assailant intends to kill you. Everyone uses these. They are like knives with a narrower blade.

2. Ceremonial. This is fancier and is usually worn as part of a uniform (*outmoded* (OMT)) and will not have changed its pattern for centuries. Be careful when you see someone with one of these. It indicates that she/he is about to attack you when you have no weapon yourself. You will, after a bout of unarmed combat, be forced to kill this person with her/his own ceremonial Dagger.

3. Mercy blades. These are spare Daggers carried in a special place by most MERCENARIES and WARRIOR WOMEN and by some DESERT NOMADS; they use the Daggers to kill themselves or their friends when survival is out of the question. Expect at least once on the Tour

to have to finish one of these people off with her/his own mercy blade, usually at the person's own request.

**DANGER** is everywhere in Fantasyland. You will be in Danger from the first step you take on your Tour, starting with the intruder with a knife on your first night, then running through ASSASSINS and DEMONS on to WIZARDS and bad QUEENS and finally the DARK LORD—not to speak of AMBUSHES in between and subtle Dangers devised by ENCHANTRESSES. You will spend a lot of time fleeing. In order not to live in a state of perpetual abject Terror, you must remember that in Fantasyland, Danger has an actual SMELL. (*REEK OF WRONG-NESS* is the general OMT for it.) Watch for this Smell. HORSES are good at detecting it. When there is any threat to safety, they have *their heads up scenting danger* (OMT). Learn to recognise what the Horses are sniffing and from then on you can relax until the moment you smell it.

**DARK LADY.** There is never one of these—so see DARK LORD instead. The Management considers that male Dark Ones have more potential to be sinister, and seldom if ever employs a female in this role. This is purely because the Management was born too late to meet my Great Aunt Clara.

**DARK LORD** (*dread lord* (OMT)). There is always one of these in the background of every Tour, attempting to ruin everything and take over the world. He will be so sinister that he will be seen by you only once or twice, probably near the end of the Tour. Generally he will attack you through MINIONS (*forces of Terror, bound to his will* (OMT)), of which he will have large numbers. When you do get to see him at last, you will not be surprised to find he is black (see COLOUR CODING) and shadowy and probably not wholly human. He will make you feel very cold and small. Actually, when it comes down to it, that is probably all he will do, having almost certainly exhausted his other resources earlier on. You should be able to defeat him, with a little help from your COMPANIONS, without too much effort. However, the Rules state that at this stage you will be exhausted yourself and possibly wounded by MAGIC. So be careful.

**DEMONS** are less frequent on the Tour than they used to be. Most of them have followed VAMPIRES and WERES over to the Horror Tour, possibly because people evoke them more there. Nevertheless, quite a few remain and must be treated with caution or, preferably, shunned. The Management itself is quite good at shunning. It is often very hard to discover what any given Demon looks like, apart from a general impression of large size, huge fangs, staring eyes, many limbs, and an odd colour; but all accounts agree that Demons are very powerful, very MAGIC (in a nonhuman manner) and made of some substance that can squeeze through a keyhole yet not be pierced with a SWORD. This makes them difficult to deal with, even on the rare occasions when they are friendly. Demons are sometimes found batting about loose, but mostly they appear to live elsewhere entirely and must therefore be invoked by NAME (often hard to pronounce) and confined within a PENTAGRAM or MAGIC circle while they are given their orders. Tourists are advised to leave all this sort of thing to WIZARDS and never, ever attempt to bargain with a Demon themselves. The Rule is that all Demons are cheats.

**DESERT** occurs very suddenly some way south—usually, but not always, at the edge of the grassy plain where the crows will SPY on you (see BIRDS). It is of course very hot and dry there, and the sand dunes roll away to the horizon like *waves*

*of a frozen sea* (OMT). When you reach the Desert, be prepared to be in it for days and to experience at least one sandstorm, either magical or natural, before you run out of WATER. Some time after that, but not until then, you will encounter someone from the DESERT NOMADS, who will usually gallop away without talking to you. Never fear. She/he has only gone to warn the rest of the CLAN that they have visitors.

One odd fact about the Desert is that, considering the unrivalled opportunities it gives for ILLUSIONS, mirages are nearly nonexistent here. No WIZARD seems yet to have got to work on this.

 **DESERT NOMADS** occupy the hot parts to the south, which is either DESERT or rather parched grass. For some reason this is ideal TERRAIN for breeding HORSES, of which all Nomad CLANS have huge numbers. The Clans move from place to place, each in their own areas, with their wondrous TENTS, flocks, and Horses, but tend to muster at least once a year for religious reasons. Desert Nomads usually have a GODDESS and are always hot on RELIGION. They also have lots of wisdom and KNOWLEDGE, much of which is in the head of the SHAMAN allotted to each Clan. Tourists will come to this PEOPLE to learn. But be prepared for two peculiarities. First, unlike the northerly Clans, Desert Nomads allow their women to do everything the men do. Second, both sexes are always *swathed from head to foot* (OMT) in ROBES, though they may have all sorts of finery underneath. They seem to have a TABOO on legs: no Nomad ever shows her/his legs in public, even when riding flat out astride a STALLION.

 **DOMESTIC ANIMALS** are as rare as wild ANIMALS. In most cases their existence can be proved only by deduction. Thus, sheep must exist, because people wear wool, and so must cattle, as there is usually cheese to eat. Cats are seen in company with WITCHES and CRONES, often in large numbers, but seldom elsewhere, and there have been sightings also of solitary pigs; possibly in Fantasyland cats are herd animals whereas pigs are not. Goats are seen oftener (and may even provide the cheese) and dogs are frequent but often rather feral—the arrival of the Tour party at a VILLAGE is usually greeted by barking dogs. Dogs are also kept in numbers by KINGS and nobles, where their job is to be scavengers: you throw bones on the floor and the dogs fight for them. These hounds cannot be kept for hunting (except perhaps for hunting men and MUTANT NASTIES), as there are no Animals to hunt.

The thoughtful Tourist might like to pause here and consider, since ANIMALS are so rare, what exactly the meat is that the Management puts in its STEW.

**DONKEYS** are rare and are reserved for the use of MONKS and humble but friendly WIZARDS. In each case the relevant APPRENTICE or NOVICE will follow on foot.

**DRAGONS** are very large scaly beings with wings and long spiky tails, capable of breathing fire through their mouths. They can be almost any colour or combination of colours, though green, red, and black are preferred. They are always very old. Most of them seem to have flown to Fantasyland aeons ago across the void. This migration was almost certainly to get away from our world, where people would insist that they were dangerous MONSTERS that had to be exterminated.

Dragons, as all Fantasyland knows, are no such thing. They quite like people, provided you can get their attention. They are very wise and can do MAGIC of a type not known to other MAGIC USERS. But they do not have human emotions.

This can cause misunderstandings, if Tourists are trying to make friends with them. Female Tourists are best at this. Dragons seem to be in tune with the female mind. A friendly Dragon will airlift female Tourists to the OFFSHORE ISLAND where most Dragons live. A male Tourist will have to wait to meet Dragons until he has been through the CAVERNS that lead to the Hidden VALLEY, where Dragons also live; or until the Dragons have joined the forces of GOOD for the Final CONFRONTATION. Even then, the relationship is likely to be a bit edgy. This is because Dragons can, if they want, eat people.

**DREAMS.** While you are on the Tour, your psyche is in the care of the Management, who will when necessary provide you with Dreams. You should always attend to these, particularly when they are repeated next night in the same form. They occupy the same slot as LEGENDS. They will be telling you something you need to know for the next phase of your Tour, but they will not be doing so very clearly. You will need to think a bit.

See also PROPHECY and VISIONS.

**DUKES.** This is the highest form of lord, often one of the KING's family. Very few of them are GOOD and most of them are wicked uncles at the very least. The few Good Dukes are always frantically busy and beset with *cares of state*(OMT). The Rule is that all Dukes, Good or EVIL, are always forty years old or more. See also REGENTS.

**DUNGEONS** are the first thing to be built when anyone is planning a large BUILDING. Even Town Halls tend to have them. The Rules state that Dungeons are damp and small and a long way underground. If the Tourist being confined is lucky, there will be a small barred window too high up to reach, through which the contents of the moat trickle, and old (*fetid* OMT, *filthy* OMT) straw on the ground. There will be a thick door (locked) with a small shutter in it where what passes (only just) for FOOD can be thrown in at prisoners, generally dropping tantalizingly an inch out of reach, and there will always be rings in the walls carrying chains and sometimes old bones too. It is all designed to make you feel low. There may even be *scutterings* OMT that could be rats (but see ANIMALS). Do not, however, let this get you down. The average stay in such a place is, for Tourists, twenty-four hours. If the Dungeon is a pit of the type called an oubliette, on the other hand, you are justified in slight melancholy. It will be several days before someone lowers a rope to you and hauls you out.

See also PRISON.

**DWARFS** are short, muscular, bearded PEOPLE much given to mining and forging. They mostly live hidden inside hills, where they do their mining. Until recently, almost no female Dwarfs had been sighted, but now they are seen quite often. They do not always have beards, but seem to be squat like the males. All Dwarfs, perhaps through living so long immured in DWARVEN FASTNESSES, have a very old-fashioned, surly demeanour. They bow a lot, but also grumble. They recite long epics about the marvellous deeds of their ancestors. The advantage of their old-fashioned ways, however, is that they are very honourable and always keep their word once they have been induced to give it. They will join the forces of GOOD and supply ARMOUR, but before this the Tour may well have a difficult time with them. Dwarfs will take all Tourists prisoner for trespassing in their Fastness, and it will involve much persuasive talking to get them to be friendly.

D

**DWARVEN FASTNESS.** A wondrous place. It normally occupies the whole inside of a MOUNTAIN. It has concealed gates, often protected by RUNES. Inside, there is gallery after gallery carved out of the Mountain, usually ornamented with Dwarven sculpture and JEWELS. It will be lit by torches or glowbaskets. There never seems to be any domestic quarter for females, children, or cooking: it is all fabulous hallways. The place is so many-levelled and labyrinthine that Tourists easily become lost there. As they blunder along, DWARFS will capture them and drag them to the Central Hall, which is often rougher and more workaday than the rest of the place. Possibly the Dwarfs keep most of it as a historical monument. On occasions, the Fastness will be deserted, long-abandoned. Here a MAP or guide is essential.

**DWELL** is the word used throughout the Tour meaning to live somewhere. The inhabitants are always *Dwellers* (OMT).

*Energies are far-reaching things. The Sage Morinden once fetched himself a lemon from a distant galaxy and felt much refreshed.*

Ka'a Orto'o,
**Gnomic Utterances,** *XIII i*

**EATING IMPLEMENTS** are minimal. The most usual provided is a SPOON for STEW. Otherwise you are expected to use your knife or DAGGER to eat with.

**ECOLOGY.** The Ecology of Fantasyland is in a bad way. It is full of empty niches. To start with, there are few or no bacteria. We can see this by the way REFUSE and other pieces of SQUALOR lie about in heaps which fail to rot down. To add to this, there are few or no INSECTS (except for fleas, some localized bees, numerous silkworms somewhere in the FANATIC CALIPHATES, and clouds of mosquitoes in the MARSHES). Both these empty niches mean that all crops will be poor; perhaps this explains the crop failures more usually blamed on MAGIC or the personality defects of KINGS. There are also very few BIRDS. In the absence of bacteria and Insects, one might expect plants and Birds to adapt so that Birds do the pollinating as well as their normal task of spreading the seeds, but this is not the case. The one species that seems to be moving into the niche normally occupied by Birds is the LEATHERY-WINGED AVIANS, but these are predators, not seedfeeders or pollinators. (And, in the absence of ANIMALS, we have to ask what exactly the Leathery-Winged Avian feeds on. Perhaps we should conjecture the existence of lots of juicy little bats? These would come forth silently at night and therefore remain largely unobserved.)

So there is no means of improving the soil, or of pollination, or of seed-spreading. Constant magical irradiation seems to have destroyed it all. It seems to have destroyed also any large wild predator mammals and most ruminants. This is a pity. These larger Animals would ordinarily do their part by spreading dung and carrying seeds in their coats. In their absence, we should not be surprised that so many TREES have become mobile: they have to move about in order to find more fertile ground and shed their seeds in it.

Plants might be expected to adapt to these conditions by evolving to become wind-pollinated. Few of them have. In the empty heathlands left by the shrinking of the VESTIGIAL EMPIRE, just where we might expect wind pollination to happen, Tour after Tour reports sparse vegetation and no food ANIMALS or BIRDS. Clearly not enough plants are getting pollinated to support small creatures here, which in turn would support larger ones. The food chains are in a bad way.

We come to the reasons for all this in the WASTE AREAS left desolate by the WIZARDS' WAR. There was fierce magical pollution here and its effects are still seeping out into the rest of the continent. Tourists who visit these sites report that the magical irradiation has resulted in hungry slimes, dark twisted plants that try to eat people in a variety of ingenious ways, and numerous highly active Animals with a taste for human flesh. This is most encouraging. All these living things—along with MONSTERS and MUTANT NASTIES—are flourishing and spreading with a strength and vitality that suggest that in time to come they will move out into all the vacant ecological niches. Fantasyland will become filled with aggressive plants and vicious animals. Humans will find themselves near the bottom of every food chain. All will be well. Unfortunately, it will be several hundred years before this happens.

E

**ECONOMY.** The Economy of Fantasyland is as full of holes as its ECOLOGY. Most areas seem self-sufficient in a hand-to-mouth, depressed way, and very poor, since WEATHER and magical pollution seem regularly to cause a shortage of food crops. But some areas, notably among the MERCHANT FEUDALISTS and the FANATIC CALIPHATES, appear to carry on considerable trade by sea and land. Both areas support large ARMIES, either MERCENARY or conscript. This shows that both have healthy trade balances. But it is hard to know where their trade comes from. PIRATES on both the open sea and the INLAND SEA make sure that few SHIPS arrive at their destination, and on land BANDITS intercept most CARAVANS. Neither Pirates nor Bandits seem to recirculate the wealth they acquire. Yet there is considerable wealth in places, for the THIEVES' GUILD is never out of business and frequently possesses itself of remarkably valuable purses and artifacts. CITIES where the Guild operates all seem to thrive. Where does the wealth come from? Now add to this the facts that two-thirds of the continent is out of action as a producer of wealth, by reason of the polluted WASTE AREAS, and that large quantities of precious metal are also out of circulation under DRAGONS, in lost treasures, or by reason of being enchanted into an unusable condition; and the mystery deepens. Add to this again the very small signs of any INDUSTRY, and one begins to ask oneself just how the Economy is maintained. The VESTIGIAL EMPIRE seems central to the mystery. Here we have a large civilized area in the centre of the landmass, with a vigorous Economy, large building programmes, faultless engineering, and full employment. But no Industry. How is this managed? One has to suppose that regular paying Tours from other worlds secretly support the whole tottering edifice.

See also IMPORT/EXPORT.

**ELEMENTALS** fairly frequently adopt visible form and sometimes even show off to Tourists. A typical Elemental is seen as a whirling cloud of dust, in or just outside the Desert. It is not clear whether this is an earth or an air Elemental. Perhaps it can be either. Elementals exist for many other things besides the earth, air, fire, and water that the Tourist will know from her/his own world, and in all categories are much more numerous. Ice Elementals are common, IRON not unknown, and Fog or MIST ones have been sighted. WIZARDS will often summon an elemental to help in their work. The preferred, but most dangerous, kind are FIRE Elementals, which can take the form of a human or ANIMAL made of flames. These, like all Elementals, are mischievous and unreliable, and can easily set everything in sight ablaze if not carefully controlled.

Most Elementals can take on quasi-human form, but Tourists are advised to refrain from chatting with them. You might put ideas into their quasi-heads that would be hard to dislodge. For instance, if you expressed pleasure in a cool breeze the Elemental would thereafter follow you around for weeks blowing half a gale.

**ELITE** are the people who, while not being PRINCES or

PRINCESSES necessarily, are nevertheless destined for great things. They have star quality. Most of them will have sprung from humble-to-medium backgrounds and will have had Sorrows. Usually they have been cast out of a CLAN, but some of them have simply been orphaned at an early age. In neither case will they tell you their troubles until you know them really well. Meanwhile, the events the Gods have chosen them for will be catching up with both of you. If an Elite joins your Tour, expect a lot of INCIDENTS.

See also MISSING HEIRS.

**ELVES** claim to have been the first PEOPLE in Fantasyland. They are called the Elder Race. They did not, they claim, evolve like humans, but sprang into being just as they are now. Certainly there seems to be no such thing as an Elvish ancestral ape, or if there was it existed too long ago for any sign of it to remain. The Elves' claim is borne out to some extent by the well-attested fact that their flesh is less gross and substantial than that of humans. This fineness of sub-stance seems to be what makes them IMMORTAL (although not invulnerable: they can be killed). In looks, Elves are taller and more slender than any humans, and very beautiful. Most of them appear youthful. Only rarely does an Elf show signs of age. Then she/he is very wise. The majority have flowing blond or ash-blond hair and huge blue-green eyes, though the odd few are dark (see COLOUR CODING). A dark Elf, even if not allied with EVIL, is likely to be even more stand-offish and equivocal in her/his attitude to humans than a fair one; but *all* Elves feel themselves superior to humans and make it very clear that they do not operate by human rules.

This is true, in that all of them can do some MAGIC, surround themselves at will with a silver or blue-green nimbus, and move freely in and out of other dimensions. But their most impressive Magic is always communal. In groups, Elves can create warded magical space, conjure meals, hollow out hills, and put on spectacular displays of riding through the air. Much of this group Magic is done by singing. All Elves sing, usually in beautiful unearthly voices. (See MUSIC and WARDS.)

Elves generally live in some sort of magical side-skewed reality, sometimes called Otherwhere or Elsewhere, which can be reached only through certain spots in WOODS, MOUNTAINS, Hidden VALLEYS, or even underwater, making them elusive and hard to encounter or study. Much of their customs, economy, and way of life is still obscure. All that is known is that Elves owe allegiance to powerful KINGS and QUEENS, who can at times be rather frightening. But Elves have made a contract with the Management that ensures that the Tourist will encounter Elves at least once on a Tour. Here you may be in for a treat. Despite fleshly differences, Elves can interbreed with humans. They may even be the only Other PEOPLE who can. And offspring seldom result, since the Elven birthrate was always low and has become lower in recent times.

In fact, Elves appear to have deteriorated generally since the coming of humans. If you meet Elves, expect to have to listen for hours while they tell you about this—many Elves are great bores on the subject—and about what glories there were in ancient days. They will intersperse their account with nostalgic ditties (*songs of aching beauty* (OMT)) and conclude by telling you how great numbers of Elves have become so wearied with the thinning of the old golden wonders that they have all departed, departed into the West. This is correct, provided you take it with the understanding that Elves do not say anything quite straight. Many Elves have indeed gone west, to Minnesota and thence to California, and finally to Arizona, where they have great fun wearing punk clothes and riding motorbikes.

**EMBROIDERY** is very frequent on CLOTHING, banners, hangings, and cushions, and badges are Embroidered on most uniforms. A lot of it is beautiful, and there is so much of it that there must be the equivalent of factories devoted to making it. But no Tour is ever taken round these. The only people the Tourist will see actually engaged in Embroidery will be ladies of high birth. And they can't do all of it. Can they?

E

**ENCHANTMENT.** This is the Management's term for manipulative MAGIC. Under its influence you will feel nice, become dreamy, and find yourself doing something you would not otherwise do. Enchantment can be worked for both GOOD and EVIL ends. For Good, it tends to be used to make trusted GUARDS leave their posts at crucial times. For Evil, it is used to make Tourists walk into a trap set by the MINIONS OF THE DARK LORD or even the DARK LORD himself.
See also ENCHANTRESS and SPELLS.

**ENCHANTRESS** is another word for "seductress," only with more punch. The one assigned to your Tour will be very beautiful, with red or black hair and probably a startling bosom, all of it magically enhanced. She will have you captured (*in her toils* (OMT)), usually by MAGIC, just over halfway through the Tour—whereupon she will proceed to seduce you if you are male; if you are female she will do something bitchily enchanting to you instead.

**ENEMY.** The marvellous thing about Fantasyland is that you nearly always know exactly who your Enemy is. Everything is black and white—there is none of the greyness that afflicts enmities in our world, where you are always having to concede that there may be some good in someone you hate. Here, Enemies are always rotten bad and also out to get Tourists, quite unequivocally. Most Enemies will of course be MINIONS OF THE DARK LORD, but some will be power-crazy WIZARDS and bad KINGS or QUEENS. You will be able to spot them at once, even if they have not yet attacked you, by their *REEK OF WRONGNESS*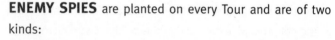. Even Enemies who are trying to be inconspicuous may be detected in this way—for instance, the UNPLEASANT STRANGER at the INN and the SPY among the CARAVAN GUARDS. All will have the Reek.

**ENEMY SPIES** are planted on every Tour and are of two kinds:

1. BIRDS, normally flocks of black crows, which will follow the Tour in open spaces such as moorland and WASTE AREAS. In DESERTS these may be replaced by vultures. Both are easy to spot but hard to defeat or avoid. They are particularly vexatious if you are trying to get somewhere secretly.

2. Humans (see also UNPLEASANT STRANGER), who are planted at INNS, usually by BANDITS, and in Courts by the DARK LORD or one of his MINIONS. These are sometimes harder to detect. Most have the *REEK OF WRONG-NESS*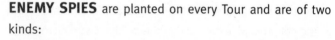, but a few will not know that it is the Dark Lord to whom they are reporting and so will not Reek. In Court, the Tourist should be wary of all who seem innocent, even if that person is the Crown PRINCE.

See also CARAVANS and SPIES.

**ETERNAL QUEST.** See QUEST, ETERNAL.

**EUNUCHS** are found very frequently, particularly in the FANATIC CALIPHATES, but also in most TEMPLES and quite often attached to WIZARDS. Wherever a KING has more than one wife, Eunuchs will abound. There are so many of them in some quarters that it must be quite a problem for the Management to maintain the birthrate high enough to provide ARMIES for bad Kings, puppet Kings, and the DARK LORD. Eunuchs do not fight. Their function is to be fat and effeminate and to thwart Tourists wherever possible by trying to POISON them. One theory is that Eunuchs are recruited from the unwanted children of barmaids (see BAR SERVICE).

**EVIL** (OMTs include *taint of Evil, Evil imperilling the realm, ancient Evil grips, Evil scheme, the Evil in men's souls, Evil springs eternal, the stench of Evil*) is generally around somewhere in Fantasyland and seems to cast quite a blight. It has two states, active and passive. In the active state, it is rampant, embodied in puppet KINGS, ARMIES of UNDEAD, MONSTERS, and creeping pollution of the countryside, and it is out to get all Tourists (who are by definition GOOD). In its passive state it ponds in deserted spots, where it lies around waiting to be aroused by the unwary. The active state is usually connected with the DARK LORD, and must be overcome in the course of the Tour. The passive, when not connected with a predecessor or avatar of the Dark Lord, is either fallout from the WIZARDS' WAR or the work of some God way back at the BEGINNING of things. When it is in this form there is not much to be done about it but stay clear.

**EXECUTIONS** are frequent in any COUNTRY not ruled by a Good KING. They take place in public in a holiday atmosphere. People flock to Executions and bring their CHIL-

E

DREN, and sales of snacks and drinks are vast. Methods of Execution are various but are generally designed to be as much of a spectacle as possible. Thus burning at the stake is a great favourite, along with impaling, crucifixion, disembowelling, etc., while suspending the victim in a cage to starve is also very popular. Hangings and beheadings, being over rather swiftly, are generally done only in batches of ten or more. Some Tours will generally include an Execution in their schedule, but on most Tours the Management wishes to spare its Tourists the sight of anything so painful. You will be irritated to find you have just missed it.

The approach to the CITY will be flanked with stakes and crosses carrying fresh corpses; its streets will be lined with severed heads or rows of throttled dangling bodies; its walls will be hung with desiccated cadavers or skeletons in small iron cages; and outside there will be large charred patches smelling of mutton chop. But you will be too late to witness anyone actually dying.

See also TORTURE.

**EXPORT.** See IMPORT/EXPORT.

**EYRIE CLANS** live in CLIFF DWELLINGS in northerly parts of the continent, where the sexes are rigidly segregated. The men live like commandoes and train BIRDS to be their lifelong companions. The women do nothing much; indeed, Tourists may not meet any of the women. The men will be very austere and humourless and not inclined to trust Tourists, but in the end they will offer their help on the side of GOOD. They make excellent scouts.

*Felt hats should be worn only before harvest time, when there is danger of bird droppings in the hair. Never wear fur boots in a marsh, and don a cloak only at great need. Do not attempt to dress like a Barbarian.*

*Ka'a Orto'o,*
**Gnomic Utterances,** *XIV ix*

**FAIRGROUND.** This is like a MARKET, except that it is much, much bigger and planted somewhere right in the middle of nowhere so that everyone can get to it. There will be rows and rows of TENTS and BOOTHS, often arranged in streets, and vast areas off to one side for HORSE trading. There will also be a profusion of JUGGLERS, Harpers (see BARDS), and other performers, all of whom will get in your way when you are trying either to find someone you urgently need to meet or to escape from SPIES and pursuers. Be sure that, if the Tour takes you to a Fairground, it will be for one of these two things. Usually it will be both.

**FANATIC CALIPHATES** generally occupy the east-southeast of the continent, where the climate is quite hot. When the Tour brings you to these COUNTRIES, you are warned to watch your tongue. They are all fanatics here in the worship of particularly demanding Gods, and are prone to TORTURE/imprison/execute anyone they regard as an unbeliever. It is this worship which enables the ruler (usually a bad KING or a TYRANT) to hold his people subject to his every word; and it is also fertile ground for the DARK LORD, who will have planted at least one puppet King here. Apart from this, the Caliphates are generally even noisier and dirtier than the rest of the continent (*clamour* OMT is expressive here), but a lot richer, which you can see at once if you walk in their MARKETS (here the OMT is *bazaar*), where they are selling carpets and silks. Everyone will be shouting about bargains and thinking of MONEY. But MERCHANTS here are thoroughly under the thumb of the King/Tyrant and will report your presence at once (and even before that if they think you have blasphemed). You will then be hustled to the PALACE. The wealth of the Country is particularly apparent in the Palace, which will be breathtakingly ornamented in a frenzy of gold, lacy jewelled carvings, wildly patterned pavements, and many-coloured cushions and hangings. There will be hundreds of well-dressed SLAVES. Here the King/Tyrant will ask you politely what you want (these people are seldom rude) and, when you reveal which QUEST OBJECT/item of KNOWLEDGE you are looking for, will take the same reasonable line as the rest of his people: "What's in it for me?" You will get nowhere unless you can answer this to everyone's satisfaction, and even then you will have to steal what you need. The Caliphates do not consider it cheating to cheat foreigners and unbelievers. You will then be pursued by fanatic soldiery or PRIESTS. Some Tour members will get wounded or killed.

**FANTASYLAND** is all the country on the MAP, usually a whole continent complete with OFFSHORE ISLANDS, and sometimes including also the OTHER CONTINENT, when this lies near enough to be reached either by Slave GALLEY or on Dragonback. There is plenty of room in it for numerous COUNTRIES, for much space to have been laid waste by earlier WIZARDS' WARS, and for still more space to be emptied by the shrinking of the VESTIGIAL EMPIRE. The WEATHER in both these emptied spaces is likely to be peculiar. The Management of course reserves the right to alter the shape and name of the continent at will and to move MOUNTAINS about whenever necessary. There will, however, always be the usual features present, as discussed in this *Toughpick* section.

**FARMHOUSES** are among the few BUILDINGS which are not larger inside than out—in fact, they are usually smaller. Outside, they are thatched, timbered, and pleasantly large-looking. Inside, there will be room only for the KITCHEN, which is the family living room, and bedrooms for the farmer, his wife and four children. Tourists invited to stay the night usually sleep in the stable loft.

**FARMING** obviously takes place, since produce appears in the MARKETS, and the Tour will sometimes take you past cultivated fields. But most fields will have been trampled or burnt by ARMIES, or else parched by magical drought. Dairy farming seems very rare. This probably accounts for the extreme dullness of most meals in Fantasyland (see STEW, FOOD, STEW, SCURVY, STEW, etc.).

**FARSEEING** can be performed by a MAGIC USER with or without a CRYSTAL, though it often takes a trance without. Here the operator lies on her/his back under a fur rug, often in some place of POWER, and during some hours sees things that are happening several hundred miles away. It is said to be very draining. The operator usually requires a hot, sweet drink afterwards.

 **FELLOW TRAVELLERS.** These are people who join the Tour for a short while and then leave or get killed. If they have NAMES and characters, then you will be sorry to lose them, otherwise not.

See also COMPANIONS.

  **FEMALE MERCENARY.** This will be a COMPANION on your Tour. She is usually tall, thin and wiry, silent, and neurotic. SEX scares her. This is because she either came from a NUNNERY or was raped as a child. Or both. Somehow this inspired her to become a MERCENARY and she is very good at her job. You can rely on her absolutely in a FIGHT. She can usually kill two people at once while guarding your back in between. The rest of the time, she will irritate you with lots of punctilious WEAPONS cleaning and a perpetual insistence that a proper watch be kept. Mostly, she will have no Magic TALENTS, but sometimes, in an emergency, she will come up with a GIFT or a VISION. You will end up grudgingly admiring her.

 **FERRY** is a raftlike craft for crossing RIVERS. It can be rowed or pulled across on ropes, but in either case the FERRYMAN must be paid. Since the Rules state that you need a Ferry only when the forces of Dark are on your heels, the price is usually exorbitant.

 **FERRYMAN** is the only important FERRY operator. All the other rowers and haulers are extras. A Ferryman is traditionally surly, reluctant, and frightened. This is probably because the Tour usually hauls him out of bed near dawn with urgent demands to be taken over the RIVER right *now*. He will overcharge you horribly in revenge. He will sometimes also blight the crossing by making various ominous and depressing remarks; but he will, on the offer of more money, swear not to reveal that you have used his Ferry. He will of course tell the forces of Dark everything as soon as they gallop up in pursuit.

**FEVER** is something that follows a wound: it never has any other cause (except possibly PLAGUE, which you will not catch). It will cost the Tourist a day or so of sweating and strange DREAMS before someone fetches a HEALER. Then a drink of herbal tea will have you right in no time.

**FIGHTS** follow the same Rules as CONFRONTATIONS and INCIDENTS. They get larger and more frequent as the Tour goes on. You will first *blood your sword* OMT in the AMBUSH mounted by the BANDITS, and follow that by further practice upon LEATHERY-WINGED AVIANS. You will then Fight an Assassin in a TOWN or CITY and so proceed by increments to your bout in the arena as a GLADIATOR. By the end of the Tour, you will be leading the front-line charge against the forces of Dark quite happily, killing soldiers, UNDEAD, and DEMONS almost with abandon.

**FIRE.** One of the very few things most forces of the Dark find hard to combat. One of the standard ways to defeat the DARK LORD or his MINIONS is to engineer a mighty explosion in the place where he/they are holed up, then let everything burn for days. Of course, before this the Dark Lord will have set Fire to large parts of the countryside, so it is only fair.

See also ELEMENTALS.

**FIRESTARTING** is one of the basic Magic TALENTS, and often manifests at an early age. This must be dangerous (see BUILDING MATERIALS), but the inhabitants of Fantasyland have learnt to take it in their stride. The Firestarter has only to concentrate for a candle or fuel in a grate to burst into flame. It is a lowly Talent. Young MAGIC USERS often apologize that this is all they can do. And thank goodness it seems confined wholly to candles and grates. We are probably lucky that in our own world it is not nearly so common.

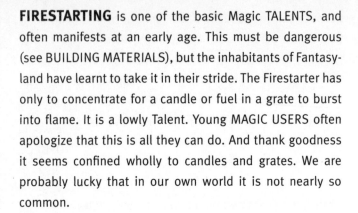

**FISH** is caught all along the coasts and often in the INLAND SEA, with much palaver about putting to sea in small wooden BOATS, mending nets and so on. It is unloaded as picturesquely as possible on to WHARFS. But it is very seldom eaten, and almost never by Tourists, except just occasionally as a variant on STEW. One conjecture is that it is carted inland to manure fields ravaged by ARMIES, WIZARDS, droughts, and demonic invasion. But this has never been confirmed. Also, trout (*plump and gleaming* OMT) may be caught in a RIVER, almost always by the FEMALE MERCENARY, who tickles out the fish *with a cocky glint in her eye* OMT; the fish are then gutted with a thumbnail and cooked on a spit over the campfire. They taste delicious, although burnt on the outside and raw in the middle.

**FLEAS.** See LICE.

**FOOD.** See STEW, SCURVY, STEW, WAYBREAD (also known as Journey Cake) and STEW—though there are occasional BIRDS, FISH, RABBITS and pieces of cheese. Generally the diet is an unvaried one, although MARSH DWELLERS can work wonders with ROOTS. Puddings are unknown except occasionally in the Courts of KINGS. Tourists who suffer from diabetes should be quite safe.

**FORESEEING.** Foreseeing is done by those MAGIC USERS with the GIFT of looking into the future, quite often MYSTICAL MASTERS. It is done unasked. Indeed, most people would rather not know. But, unlike the other forms of PROPHECY, this is usually very obscure, although quite accurate. Tourists should not lose sleep over it. Whatever is Foreseen is going to happen anyway.

**FOREST OF DOOM.** This is usually the home of mobile and prehensile TREES. There will be giant SPIDERS too, and Dwellers near the centre who will want to SACRIFICE any stranger to their God. It is best to avoid the place if possible. But the Management usually insists on sending you there. An OLD RUINED CITY is sometimes situated in the heart of this Forest.

See also WOODS.

**FORTS** usually occur in MOUNTAINS. Generally they are guarding a pass, but sometimes they are just there. They are about equally divided between manned and deserted. In all cases they are sort of square and blockish, with many additional geometric features for which the Management seldom gives reasons. The Rule is that if a Fort is manned, then it will be attacked by the forces of the Dark. If it is deserted, then some SECRET vital to the Tour QUEST is concealed there.

**FROSTBITE** is unknown, even in the extreme frozen north. This is convenient for Tourists, who will be compelled to suffer HARDSHIPS of cold when visiting the north, and also

probably accounts for the fact that the NORTHERN BARBAR-
IANS wear little besides a furry loincloth.

See also CHILBLAINS and HYPOTHERMIA.

**FRUIT** is probably a luxury item. It is seldom served at INNS
and usually makes its appearance only at feasts in the courts
of KINGS.

See also SCURVY.

**G**

*Gardens are fraught with risk. King Doras II fell over a flowerpot in his garden after seeing a vision of seven future kings.*

Ka'a Orto'o,
**Gnomic Utterances,** *I ix*

**GALLEY.** A large, cumbrous SHIP moved by both sail and banks of oars. Usually, but not invariably, it belongs to the FANATIC CALIPHATES, who may be using it for trade. Or maybe not, because the only things most Galleys seem to contain are rows of benches for GALLEY SLAVES.

**GALLEY SLAVE.** The only opportunity, if you are a man, of reaching any of the OFFSHORE ISLANDS is to become a Galley Slave. It is one of the two main occupations open to you once you are enslaved (see also GLADIATOR). You will be captured and sold into slavery on an average halfway through the Tour and will then very shortly find yourself chained to a bench belowdecks (*noisome* OMT) and probably to a large heavy oar too. (There is no toilet provided, hence the OMT.) You have to sit there all the time, even when the galley is under sail. You will be given just enough food and drink to keep you alive. There will be an overseer (*brutal* OMT) who will encourage you with a large leather whip, as well as someone else to beat time as you row. You will find it hard work. You will acquire blisters and scars as well as muscles. But do not despair. Next to you on the bench there will be a future friend, generally of giant stature, and, as soon as your muscles are properly hardened, you will be able to cut your chains and, with the help of this LARGE MAN, slaughter your employers and leap overboard. You may then have to swim some way to an island. If you are lucky, a SEA MONSTER will arise from the deep and offer you a lift, but even without this help you will reach land in a day or so. In some cases, you may find that you have not reached an island at all, but some other land. This will be the OTHER CONTINENT and the Tour will proceed as normal there.

**GAMES** are few, usually only dice, cards, and chess.

GUARDS, soldiers, and Thieves are all addicted to dice, which they normally play only when drinking. This is a convenient habit, since it will often enable you to slip past them, either into or out of a PRISON, FORT, or TOWN, whenever you need to. Often the dice have been crafted from unusual materials, like human vertebrae, and they may have RUNES on them in place of the normal spots.

Card games are always fraught affairs, since inevitably the fall of the cards has some *miasma of meaning* **(OMT)** that goes far beyond the game itself; players are likely to look over their shoulders nervously before reluctantly muttering "Snap."

Chess seems to be played by the upper classes. That is to say, you will find KINGS, rich MERCHANTS, and the like all possess very handsome chess sets, but you will almost never see them playing with them.

Psychiatrists may find matter for grave concern in the

F
G

almost total absence of other Games, particularly among children, but the reason is easy to find. From the cradle up, the inhabitants are in the serious business of keeping alive in spite of the best efforts of the DARK LORD, WIZARDS, bad Kings, DEMONS, and maverick MAGIC, and have no time for fripperies.

See also GAMING.

**GAMING** is done with dice by soldiers and SPIES. Dice are traditionally loaded. Tourists are not advised to try it.

See also GAMES.

**GAY MAGE** may be one of your COMPANIONS on the Tour. He will be very beautiful and he will dress in gorgeous colours. He will have long hair which may be silver-blond. He will *ache with sensitivity*(OMT). He will not like to fight or to be angry with people. Despite all this, he will be surprisingly strong, competent, and determined, and he will be very good at MAGIC indeed. He will fall in love while on the Tour and suffer other disasters, but this will not impair his efficiency in the least. You will find him giving you a back rub and aromatherapy late in the Tour at some point when he ought to be dead. A valuable Companion.

**GEAS** is the word for the Rules governing PanCeltic TOURS. On normal PanCeltic Tours it is something magically laid on you that you must do or not do. This can be a nuisance, because the Geas takes no account of the feelings you may have about whatever is laid on you. For instance, you can be under a Geas to marry the next person you see with violet eyes, or to kill every third red-haired man, or to visit every COUNTRY on the MAP, and you will do those things. You may weep and curse, but do them you will.

**GESTURES** are the invariable accompaniment to the performing of MAGIC. The Management here takes the reasonable line that, without Gestures, most people would not know that Magic was being done. So all WIZARDS wave their arms about a lot. Many Gesture with their STAFFS. Some flick their fingers. In extreme cases, the Gesture leaves a *green glowing trace in the air* (OMT).

**GHOSTS** come both singly and in battalions. Single Ghosts are met in MANSIONS and out of doors, but very seldom in CASTLES, PALACES, or other places where people might have come by sticky ends. This is because Ghosts on the whole seem to exist not as a result of the way they died but because of unfinished business. This applies particularly to Ghosts in battalions, who will be waiting in a large cemetery or graveyard for someone to call them up to fulfil their vows. Single Ghosts will be feeling vengeful about some legal or magical matter they have had to leave to their descendants. Tourists should be careful of all Ghosts. In Fantasyland, Ghosts can interact with living substance and do real damage. Single Ghosts can hurt or bespell you. The called-up battalions usually fight like living soldiers but are, for obvious reasons, very difficult to kill.

**GIANTS** are seldom seen these days. They may be invisible (see INVISIBILITY). If you think you see a Giant, it will usually prove to be a very large human or the result of a BREEDING PROGRAMME. There are, however, confirmed sightings of a whole race of gentle Giants. Tours occasionally stumble on these.

**GIFTS** is another word for TALENTS. It is used by people who feel reverent about MAGIC.

**GLADIATOR** is the second of two professions open to male Tourists when they are taken prisoner and sold as a SLAVE (see also GALLEY SLAVE). You need not be muscular for this, though it helps; it is better to have a brain and to have recently been in WEAPONS training at a SCHOOL OF WEAPONRY (the Management usually arranges for this to have been the case). Once enslaved, you will be taken to the pitlike pens at the back of the arena, where you will be lightly chained but not underfed or too badly treated, since your owners wish you to give the audience a decent show. You may even be allowed exercise. During this time, you will hear rumours about the other Gladiators, the professionals, one of whom will be said to have defeated all comers. Naturally, when your time comes to fight, this will be the man you have to meet. With luck, you will by this time have had a few early bouts, either with other professionals or with a mutant ANIMAL or two, and your skills will be honed. But this fight will be the big one. Often, freedom will be the reward. The Rule is: if you are offered freedom, then you must kill your professional; but if you are just put to fight him, you will get the best of it and the man will become your friend. The two of you will then escape together.

But either way, you have to fight him, in glaring heat (this is the Rule) and in front of the local TYRANT and a huge crowd. Usually your opponent will have superior WEAPONS. But thanks to your earlier training you are able, at the last gasp, to pull a fast one on him and win. The crowd will then wish you to take his place as their HERO. This can be awkward, but do not worry. The Rule is that you can escape during the next day or so.

**GNOMES** are a small, brown, rather childish PEOPLE who tend to live beneath the roots of TREES or under hillsides.

F
G

They come out of their earthy warrens to capture Tourists for no real reason. Since they have some knowledge of MAGIC they can make life uncomfortable and be hard to escape from. Nor do they always understand that humans need to eat and drink. Captured Tourists are advised to work hard at finding out what the Gnomes want, or think they want, and then talking them out of it. The average time this takes is about forty-eight hours. By this time you are very hungry and thirsty indeed.

**GNOMIC UTTERANCES.** These are traditional, and are set at the head of each section of the Guidebook. The reason for them is lost in the mists of HISTORY. They are culled by the Management from a mighty collection of wise sayings probably compiled by a SAGE—probably called Ka'a Orto'o—some centuries before the Tour begins. The Rule is that no Utterance has anything whatsoever to do with the section it precedes. Nor, of course, has it anything to do with GNOMES.

**GOBLINS** are the smaller unmutated form of ORCS, and quite as unpleasant. They are *misshapen* (OMT) ugly humanoids with long nails and teeth. Usually they have green scaly skins and pointed ears. They live underground in MOUNTAINS and WOODS and are likely to pour out of these dens in hundreds and attack the Tour without warning. They have a habit of keeping on coming, however many you kill, so you will find you have to keep cutting Goblins to pieces until your arm aches. If there are enough Goblins, they will capture you at this stage and haul you underground. It will be some days before your COMPANIONS manage to rescue you. Be prepared for a bad few days. Goblins enjoy TORTURE and are rather good at it. Some Goblins are cannibals too.

**GODDESSES AND GODS** operate in ones, threesomes, or whole pantheons of nine or more (see RELIGION). Most of them claim to have made the world, and this is indeed a likely claim in the case of threesomes or pantheons: Fantasyland does have the air of having been made by a committee. But all Goddesses and Gods, whether they say they made the world or not, have very detailed short-term plans for it which they are determined to carry out. Consequently they tend to push people into the required actions by the use of coincidence or PROPHECY, or just by narrowing down your available choices of what to do next: if a deity is pushing you, things will go miserably badly until there is only one choice left to you.

Deities are also much given to manifesting and taking part in the action themselves. They manifest, according to their natures, as a CHILD, a bright light, a silver beam, a demonic creature, or a superhuman human, and in this form will tell you what your next move must be. They have to do this. Because of the Rule that all Goddesses and Gods fade when not worshipped (see IMMORTALS), each deity has constantly to make it quite clear to humans that She/He exists. You may therefore expect to meet at least one deity during your Tour. The experience is generally awe-inspiring and usually instructive, though you may come away from it feeling rather bullied.

See also ASPECT and BEGINNINGS.

**GOOD** means everyone and everything on your side. This of course includes TOUR COMPANIONS—in spite of irritating quirks—DRAGONS, DWARFS, ELVES, and, once you have talked to them seriously, GNOMES. It means about half the GODDESSES AND GODS. Most other things are the ENEMY, and EVIL. If you find something/someone that is neither, such as a HORSE or a neutral God, you may safely ignore them.

**GOVERNMENT** in Fantasyland is another word for KING or TYRANT. Most AVERAGE FOLK seem to get on perfectly well without any of it.

See also POLITICS.

**GREEN MAN** is either a sort of walking tree composed of twigs (**OMT** *wythes*) and leaves, or a large construct woven of twigs and leaves. Nobody knows what this creature is, but it is generally acknowledged that he is very folklorique. In either form, he is highly menacing. The walking kind is liable to come after you in the night, rustling villainously and exuding the well-known *REEK OF WRONGNESS* **OMT** If you encounter the constructed form, you must run away at once, or you will likely find yourself chained inside the vegetation and then burnt, or thrown into the sea, or both. In the last case, you have at least some chance of escaping, provided you are not roast meat by then.

**GRIMOIRES** are books of EVIL SPELLS. Tourists should avoid looking into or even touching them except in true need. Most of them behave like conscious entities and are out to entrap. You can tell which they are, because their leather covers are either black or the *glabrous hue* **OMT** of human skin. Sometimes this smokes a little when fingered. Grimoires will often flutter their pages enticingly, or fall open at a Spell that entraps; but it is also quite customary for the page you need to be blank when you first look at it, or to blank itself as you try to read. If you really need to consult a Grimoire as part of your QUEST for KNOWLEDGE, you need a shielding Spell, a coercion Spell, and a Spell that enables you to remember what you saw without having nightmares for the rest of the Tour. It is best to let your Tour MENTOR or a WIZARD handle it.

**GUARDS** are the TOWN Watch and quite useless. They always arrive too late to quell a TAVERN BRAWL or riot. This is because there are too few of them and all of them are stupid. Tourists will be glad of both these facts at the point when they are trying to leave the Town unseen.

**GUILDS.** See ASSASSINS, GUILD OF and THIEVES' GUILD.

**GUNS** are banned on most Tours. If a Tourist succeeds in smuggling a Gun through from our own world, the Management will usually arrange for it not to work for some reason. On most Tours, gunpowder does not explode. If you really feel you must bring a Gun (and who is to blame you, given the trials and DANGERS of the Tour?), your best chance of getting away with it is to import something antique such as a musket or a flintlock pistol.

*Hard on your port a bit*
*Down on your right a bit*
*That's how to make a hit*
*Down with the rest of it.*

**Barbary Viking Song***

*The Management regrets that it was unable to find a Gnomic Utterance that was suitably irrelevant. It was forced to resort to doggerel instead.

**HARDSHIP** is intrinsic to all Tours. Be prepared to be cold, tired, wet, wounded, and, above all, sleepless, and still have to slog on. For some reason, sleep is the thing the Management is least prepared to allow you. But you will lose more than sleep before the CONCLUSION. Be prepared to have to go about SAVING THE WORLD with one leg or your soul missing. Until you have done this, you will not know what Hardship is.

**HARES** are a distinct species from RABBITS, which they superficially resemble—about as close to a Rabbit as a monkey is to a human—but the Management will always try to kid you that they are the same thing. Hares do not dig burrows, but spend all their life above ground, running very hard. This is probably why they so often end up in Tourist traps. Because of their lifestyle, Hares taste bitter and their flesh is so tough that they should be hung for at least two days after slaughter. The Management, however, will want you to eat the Hare that same evening and will therefore call it a Rabbit. That night's STEW will be unpleasant and very hard to chew.

**HARP.** A triangular stringed instrument, often MAGIC. Even when not Magic, a Harp is surprisingly portable and tough and can be carried everywhere on the back of the BARD or Harper in all weathers. A Harp seldom goes out of tune and never warps. Its strings break only in very rare instances, usually because the Harper is sulking or crossed in love. This is just as well, as no one seems to make or sell spare strings. If Magic, a Harp makes its player able to do most things a WIZARD can do, only few Harpers seem to realize this. Perhaps this is a pity, because almost no Harp, Magic or not, will respond to anyone who is not GOOD.

**HARPER.** See BARDS, HARP, and PanCelts.

**HEALERS** are the medics of Fantasyland, but even more highly venerated. Usually they deserve respect. They are slender, mild-mannered people who dare not kill or offer violence because this would destroy their Healing Powers. Any Healer who reverses the flow of energy to hurt instead of heal is said to suffer terribly. A Healer will show a GIFT at an early age, whereupon she/he will be taken and trained in a Hall, which seems to be something like a MONASTERY, and will emerge around the age of twenty able to close WOUNDS with a touch of the finger, dispel FEVER by concentrating, and mend bones by going into a light trance. A Healer may also know HERBS and save her/himself the fatigue of falling into a trance by applying leaves and ointments instead. Some ointments even mend broken bones. Healers appear to derive their POWER and some of their training from the hand of the GODDESS, and are often very devout people. All this makes you see that medicine in our world has a long way to go.

**HEATING** is open fires or nothing, except in MONASTERIES, TEMPLES, and the PALACES of sick KINGS, where a charcoal brazier is allowed to the abbot, HIGH PRIEST, or King. Sometimes the inside of an ANCIENT ENGINEERING PROJECT will be kept inexplicably warm by *some preternatural agency beyond the ken of Man* (OMT), indicating that the ancients knew a thing or two about central heating.

**HEATSTROKE** is rare but, since it is caused by the sun and not by bacteria, it can happen. Expect to be smitten by it in the DESERT. It will cause you only a day or so of acute discomfort.

**HEDGE WIZARD.** A MAGIC USER who received little or no training or was not intelligent enough to qualify for the College of Wizardry (see INVISIBLE COLLEGE), but who has decided to make a living out of it all the same. Most Hedge WIZARDS are small, shabby, and self-deprecating. They are to be met trudging around the land touting for custom. Tourists often feel sorry for them, and this is a snare. Few of them are EVIL, but they will land you in trouble anyway, because their SPELLS are likely to be weak or incomplete and will fail you just when you need to rely on them. Consult a Hedge Wizard only when no other help is around.

See also HERBWOMAN.

**HEIRS.** See MISSING HEIRS.

**HELMETS** are allowed only to the following, and never to Tourists:

1. GUARDS, particularly of the TOWN Watch, so they can shove the Helmet back and scratch their heads.
2. Vestigial Imperialists (see VESTIGIAL EMPIRE), so that it can be surmounted by a plume of dyed horsehair.
3. BARBARY VIKINGS, to carry the necessary horns.
4. The forces of the DARK LORD, so that they can have the visors down and behave like automata (*faceless* **OMT**).
5. Foreigners, so that they can be a peculiar foreign shape.
6. Just occasionally ARMIES, if the Management is intending to pour boiling oil on the besiegers.

**HERALDRY** is rampant, passant, and even couchant, but the exact rules are vague. Generally the Management is happy to paint an ANIMAL or plant of one colour on a field of another and leave it at that.

**HERBS** are plentiful in Fantasyland. All the most useful and curative plants seem to have escaped the magical pollution that has so blighted ANIMAL life and, what is more, whole crops of hitherto unknown healing Herbs are also available, growing freely on hillsides and the banks of streams just where and when they are needed. All HEALERS and HERB-WOMEN are well versed in their uses and habitats (*lore* **OMT**). If you are wounded, one of these can soon put you right with a poultice of crushed leaves.

**HERBWOMAN.** Said to be the female equivalent of a HEDGE WIZARD, but this is seldom the case. She is never rich, but she can be any age, and the older she is the more likely she is to be an accomplished midwife. She will usually wear HOMESPUN Robes. If young, she may join your Tour. A Herbwoman will have had little or no formal training, but she will have received enormous amounts of *lore* **OMT**

**H**

from her predecessors, and anything to do with the natural world is an open book to her. She will be quite a powerful WITCH and often able to Heal when normal HEALERS have given up. She is also likely to have LEGENDS and other KNOWLEDGE you need.

See also HERBS.

**HEROES.** These are mythical beings, often selected at birth, who perform amazing deeds of courage, strength, and magical mayhem, usually against huge odds. The Rule is that the Hero is always Out There. If you get to meet a so-called Hero, she/he always turns out to be just another human, with human failings, who has happened to be in the right place at the right time (or the wrong place at the wrong time, more likely). Tourists, too, may perform amazing deeds and quite normally end up SAVING THE WORLD, but cannot qualify as Heroes because they are not Out There.

**HIDDEN KINGDOM.** Usually reached through CAVERNS or after an arduous trek into the heart of the central massif, this is often the object of the Tour QUEST and much of the Tour will be devoted to getting directions to find it. When you get there you will discover it is very beautiful and very orderly. The Dwellers will be either MYSTICAL MASTERS or ELVES, or both. The ruler, who will be grave, wise, and comely, will talk to you long and seriously about MAGIC and your aims in life. People will play fine, restful MUSIC. You will be able to relax and feast. One good thing about this place is that they will either not serve STEW or, if they do, it will be strangely spiced and vegetarian. For a few days, you will think this is the perfect place, but after that you will be anxious to leave because it is really very boring. The Dwellers want you gone too. They find you unrestful. So they will give you a magical preview of what you do next (see PROPHECY) and fresh supplies of WAYBREAD and send you on your way to SAVING THE WORLD.

**HIEROGLYPHS** can be the form of writing used in the OTHER CONTINENT, or else a difficult and unpleasant alternative to RUNES. WIZARDS write Hieroglyphs a lot on floors and in the air. You need help to read them.

See also GRIMOIRES and SCROLLS.

**HIGH KING** is the top KING of whatever number of COUNTRIES, dukedoms, and principalities the Management pleases. He is a northerly phenomenon and does not occur on all Tours. When he does, he is always GOOD, rather conscientious, and terribly overworked. You will often witness the start of his reign about halfway through the Tour. There will be a long and tedious ceremony in which all lesser rulers swear oaths to the High King. He will then be the one who has to muster an ARMY to fight the forces of the DARK LORD.

**HIGH PRIEST** is nearly always EVIL, either on his own account or on behalf of the DARK LORD. Sometimes he is fat, thick-lipped, and corrupt, sometimes tall, thin, shaggy-browed, and corrupt. He will be wearing ROBES of enormous richness and a medallion round his neck that can shoot MAGIC at people. He has not cut his fingernails in years. Mostly he does not believe in his God, but cynically uses both the God's powers and his own considerable Magic skills to his own ends, which are (a) getting rich, (b) being cruel, and (c) acquiring catamites and concubines. The younger members of the Tour are not safe from him. He is particularly dangerous because he can call on two kinds of Magic and after that hundreds of fanatic soldiers and worshippers, who may pursue the Tour party for miles.

See also RELIGION, SCROLLS, and TEMPLES.

**HIGH PRIESTESSES** are always devout and always head the worship of female deities. They are:

1. Of the Triple Goddess. This High Priestess is good-looking, with a nice figure and a warm and motherly nature. She will give you excellent advice and any other help you need.
2. Of any other Goddess. This High Priestess is tall, thin, and austere. In her view, nothing comes before her duty to her deity. Consequently, you have to convince her that her deity wants what you need. Then she will put the large resources of her TEMPLE/COUNTRY at your service. On occasion, however, the DARK LORD has got in before you, often by pretending to be the GODDESS, and convinced the High Priestess she needs to support him. You will have to persuade her otherwise, often by trickery. But she has not got where she is by being stupid, so you will have your work cut out.

**HISTORY** is generally patchy and unreliable. Any real information about past events is either lost or contained in a SCROLL jealously guarded in a MONASTERY or TEMPLE. All that can be ascertained with any certainty is:

1. That there once was an Empire that ruled the continent from coast to coast (give or take a few enclaves of ELVES, GOBLINS, and the like), but that this shrank to one CITY a long time before the era of the current Tour, leaving only a few ROADS, perhaps some of the less ancient ANCIENT ENGINEERING PROJECTS and much deserted country.

2. That there was once a WIZARDS' WAR which probably occurred earlier still. The result of this is that large tracts of land are still magically devastated (see WASTE AREAS). See LEGENDS, as more reliable sources of information.

**HOMESPUN** (*serviceable* OMT) is probably a kind of tweed worn by those who are not rich. The cloth seems to be a sort of mud color.

**HORSE-BREEDING** is practised by both the ANGLO-SAXON COSSACKS in the mid-north and the DESERT NOMADS in the south. They are not in competition with one another and their activities do not result in a glut of horseflesh. In Fantasyland, the mortality rate for HORSES is even higher than that for MONSTERS and humans. Despite these grim statistics, both races are said to love their Horses passionately.

**HORSES** are of a breed unique to Fantasyland. They are capable of galloping full-tilt all day without a rest. Sometimes they do not require food or water. They never cast shoes, go lame, or put their hooves down holes, except when Management deems it necessary, as when the forces of the DARK LORD are only half an hour behind. They never otherwise stumble. Nor do they ever make life difficult for Tourists by biting or kicking their riders or one another. They never resist being mounted or blow out so that their girths slip, or do any of the other things that make horses so chancy in this world. For instance, they never shy and seldom whinny or demand sugar at inopportune moments. But for some reason you cannot hold a conversation while riding them. If you want to say anything to another Tourist (or vice versa), both of you will have to rein to a stop and stand staring out over a VALLEY while you talk. Apart from this inexplicable quirk, Horses can be used just like bicycles, and usually are. Much research into how these exemplary animals come to exist has resulted in the following: no mare ever comes into season on the Tour and no STALLION ever shows an interest in a mare; and few Horses are described as geldings. It therefore seems probable that they breed by pollination. This theory seems to account for everything, since it is clear that the creatures do behave more like vegetables than mammals. It also explains why the ANGLO-SAXON COSSACKS and the DESERT NOMADS appear to have a monopoly on horse-breeding. They alone possess the secret of how to pollinate them.

See also HORSE-BREEDING.

**HOVELS** are small squalid dwellings, either in a VILLAGE or occasionally up a MOUNTAIN, and probably most resemble huts. The people who live in Hovels are evidently rather lazy and not very good with their hands, since in no cases have any repairs ever been done to these buildings (*tumble-down* (OMT), *rotting thatch* (OMT), etc.) and there is no such thing as a clean Hovel. Indoors, the occupants *eke out a wretched existence* (OMT), which you can see they would, given the draughts, smoke, and general lack of house-cleaning. This need not alarm you. The Tour will not require you to enter a Hovel that is inhabited. If you enter one at all, it will be *long-deserted* (OMT) and there will be sanitary arrangements out the back.

**HYPOTHERMIA** is a very rare condition, but may be experienced by the unlucky Tourist, usually when crossing a MOUNTAIN (see MOUNTAIN PASS, BLOCKED). The cure is swift, involving hot soup and the attentions of a HEALER in an icy cave.

*Insights are always valuable, even if they only show you your duodenal ulcer.*

Ka'a Orto'o,
**Gnomic Utterances,** *V xciii*

**IDOL.** A statue of a bad or EVIL God, usually found in a TEMPLE, but occasionally carried through the streets by fanatical worshippers (see also IMAGE). It will be covered with gold, JEWELS, and caparisons, and be very ugly. The most appalling RITES and SACRIFICES will be held in front of it. On occasion an Idol will be hollow and thus usable by GOOD people as a convenient place to hide, notably if they were about to be the subject of one of those appalling Rites and Sacrifices. Oddly, through all the centuries during which they have had it, the Idol's worshippers have never noticed that it is not solid, and thus haven't a clue where you might have vanished to.

On the rare occasions when the hollowness *is* known about, the hollow space is of course used by PRIESTS to create special effects, such as a thunderous voice issuing from the Idol, the rolling of its eyes, and the belching from its mouth of flames to terrify and convince its worshippers.

**ILLUSION** is an important branch of MAGIC. In fact, some Tours work on the assumption that all Magic is really Illusion, or the art of making one thing/person seem like something quite different. Even where this is not the case, forms of Illusion play a large part. These are:

1. An appearance put on something from outside. Here the MAGIC USER makes thin air, a table, or an ARMY look like, respectively, a flight of butterflies, the REGENT, or a bank of MIST.
2. Something is done to the mind of the onlooker to make her/him see thin air, a table, or an Army as butterflies, the Regent, or a bank of Mist. This is where it can get edgy. Nasty Illusions can be planted permanently in a mind so that the person has a case of perpetual magical DTs. Worse still, the person can spend the rest of her/his life thinking she/he is an elephant or a bat.
3. Most Illusion is probably a mix of the two kinds.

**IMAGE.** A statue of a GODDESS OR GOD, only here—unlike the case with an IDOL—the deity is said to be GOOD. There will be Rites but not SACRIFICES.

**IMMORTALS** are fairly common in Fantasyland. There are three kinds:

1. GODDESSES AND GODS, who exist forever unless people stop believing in them.
2. ELVES or DARK LORDS, who live forever unless someone kills them.
3. Humans who are
   A) Cursed and have to spend Eternity drearily Questing and/or hating everything. (See CURSES and QUEST.)
   B) MAGIC USERS. These generally find plenty to occupy the long years and mostly have rather a good time.

**IMPERIAL CITIZENS** are so civilized that they have given up WAR in favour of POLITICS and POISON. The Management considers this effete and will direct you to feel contempt for most of these people, except the Emperor, until you come upon the elderly man who retains the old virtues of the Empire. A former General, he is totally trustworthy and warlike and scorns politics too. He will become a staunch supporter of the Tour and of great help either on the QUEST or in SAVING THE WORLD.

**IMPERIAL CITY.** See VESTIGIAL EMPIRE.

**IMPERIOUS FEMALE** is a Tour COMPANION you probably hate at first. She is rather finely dressed and may have the SERIOUS SOLDIER as her bodyguard. She will sweep into the INN at the STARTING POINT and behave as if what she wants is the only thing of importance to anyone. Before long, however, you will see that she is really *driven by huge anxiety* (OMT). She has some KNOWLEDGE or SECRET with her that preys on her mind, usually by suggesting her duty is SAVING THE WORLD. You will then discover she is a WITCH or of Royal birth or both. After that she will earn your respect by not complaining at any of the HARDSHIPS of the Tour, and then by rescuing everyone from either an attack by DEMONS or the efforts of a bad KING to imprison you all. And after that, she will indeed Save the World, with a little help from her friends.

**IMPORT/EXPORT** of goods clearly happens, or there would not be BALES on WHARFS. But most goods seem purely local, except perhaps in the FANATIC CALIPHATES and among the MERCHANT FEUDALISTS, where things from overseas do occasionally appear. It is not known what the

Caliphates send in exchange or where these goods are sent.

See also ECONOMY.

**INCENSE** is much used, probably because all SMELLS in Fantasyland are significant in some way. It seems to have a strong effect on everyone, particularly Tourists. When EVIL, Incense is used by ENCHANTRESSES and WITCHES and in TEMPLES; the OMTs are *heavy, soporific, seductive*, etc. When GOOD, it will be used by the GAY MAGE and referred to by what it was made from, as lavender, camomile, aniseed, pine, etc.

**INCIDENTS** should happen at regular intervals on every Tour. You should not be able to travel more than fifty miles without something happening. Usually they start small and work up to big.

1. Small Incidents include: AMBUSH (by BANDITS or LEATHERY-WINGED AVIANS); BETRAYAL; arrest by Imperial GUARDS; attack by prehensile TREES; SEX with a Tour COMPANION; an encounter with a WIZARD/ DRAGON/MINION OF THE DARK LORD/Fortune Teller; bad WEATHER; crossing a RIVER; an arrow shot suddenly from nowhere (it will miss everyone and stick in a tree); stealing something from a MONASTERY/TEMPLE; a near-fatal visit from VAMPIRES in the night; stumbling into QUICKSAND. . . .

2. Medium-Sized Incidents can be: magical STORMS; attack by small APELIKE CANNIBALS or inferior DE-MONS; being caught in crossfire during a WIZARDS' argument; capture by an ENCHANTRESS/PIRATES/PRIESTS/ NORTHERN BARBARIANS; being hunted by MINIONS OF THE DARK LORD or PRIESTS; losing your FOOD

supply; visiting a KING; becoming lost in CAVES; imprisonment/TORTURE; being enslaved as a GLADIATOR and having to FIGHT in the arena....

3. Medium-Big Incidents often concern: large DEMONS; SIEGES/battles, but not of a conclusive nature; intervention of DRAGONS/WIZARDS/GODDESSES AND GODS/ STONE CIRCLES; entrapment by a puppet KING; confrontation with an ENCHANTRESS/high MINION OF THE DARK LORD; losing your soul/SWORD/COMPANIONS; major MAGIC, resulting in earthquakes/volcanic activity/other large destructions; the opposition stealing your QUEST OBJECT....

4. Big Incidents are anything involving the end of the DARK LORD/world/both together. You do not get these until you have taken at least two previous Tours.

**INDUSTRY.** Apart from a bit of pottery and light metalwork,  or some slagheaps around the domain of the DARK LORD, most Tours encounter no Industry at all. Even EMBROIDERY factories are kept well out of sight.

See also ECONOMY.

**INFORMATION.** See KNOWLEDGE.

**INLAND SEA.** There is always one of these somewhere  around the midpoint of the continent. Tourists must expect to have to embark upon it at some stage in the Tour. It has PIRATES, but few or no SEA MONSTERS. Because it is shallower than the OUTER OCEAN, voyaging on it will be very choppy. Also, maybe because the land is all round it, it is extremely susceptible to both normal STORMS and STORM CONTROL. Expect a miserable voyage ending in capture and enslavement, or in shipwreck, or at the very least a frantic race in which your MAGIC USER tries to keep your SHIP ahead of the pursuit.

**INNKEEPERS** are all so alike that the Tourist may be pardoned for thinking she/he has not moved from one INN to the next. Innkeepers are tall, fat, male, aproned, busy, and normally jovial. They are there to serve and shout orders to barmaids. They take everything in their stride, from STRANGE RACES and TAVERN BRAWLS to peculiar requests from Tourists with awkward SECRETS to conceal. They seldom otherwise intrude on the action. They are always too busy. It is not known when these admirable men find time to eat or sleep.

**INNS** exist in TOWNS and CITIES, but seldom outside them, except at crossroads that are miles from anywhere. They are quite large buildings, mostly of wood, and are always larger upstairs than downstairs. Downstairs there is space for only the taproom and bar—a low-ceilinged CHAMBER with a fireplace at each end, the bar at one side and many tables and benches—and a KITCHEN off the back; but upstairs there is space for innumerable *sleeping chambers* OMT for the Tour party, plus whatever rooms the INNKEEPER and his staff use, all arranged around long corridors so that people can creep from one to the other and intruders can invade the rooms of Tourists either to search their baggage or to menace them with DAGGERS. There are also extensive cellars, but these are only rarely brought into the action. Outside, there will be a yard and stables for the HORSES. Sometimes, the prudent Tourist will stay in the stable with her/his Horse. It is generally a lot safer. Quite a lot of INCIDENTS tend to happen in Inns.

See also BAR SERVICE and PATRONS OF INNS.

## WHAT TO ORDER AT AN INN

The short answer is Nothing. When you arrive, the Innkeeper will bustle out and offer to show you to your Chamber at once. He will assume that you will then come downstairs to the taproom, where you will be served with Beer and Stew and, possibly, some bread. It is no good saying that you don't like Beer and would rather have milk. Inns do not stock milk. And the same applies to desserts. It is no good, either, going to your Chamber and trying to eat the chocolate you have sneaked into your baggage. You have to stay in the taproom, or you will coincide with the Intruder who will be busy searching your baggage. You will not wish to interrupt her/him, because she/he will have a knife.

**INN SIGNS** are always *crudely painted*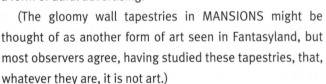. Art—except the sort of obscenely decadent art you may encounter on a TEMPLE wall and turn away from with an embarrassed wince—does not seem to be studied by the inhabitants of Fantasyland, possibly because they are usually so busy fighting and coping with magically induced CATACLYSMS. Do not be surprised to find that every Inn Sign creaks loudly. This is a form of aural advertising.

(The gloomy wall tapestries in MANSIONS might be thought of as another form of art seen in Fantasyland, but most observers agree, having studied these tapestries, that, whatever they are, it is not art.)

**INSCRIPTIONS** are widespread. Tourists will need to keep someone on hand who can *decipher* such things. They can be in RUNES, HIEROGLYPHS, or ordinary writing, but the Rule is that they are always hard to read. Although only about forty percent of Inscriptions prove to be important, you can never tell until you know what they say. Inscriptions occur:

1. On AMULETS and COINAGE. Only about half of these are significant. If an Amulet is Inscribed with the NAME of its maker, this is some guide to its MAGIC strength and efficiency. Your TOUR MENTOR will know. Coinage will have a picture of the last or current KING and an Inscription that gives his name and dates. It is surprising how often this King's profile will resemble that of a young woman on the Tour, and thus give you a clue to her identity.

2. In stone, on DWARVEN FASTNESSES, CITADELS, and TOMBS. Two-thirds of these are the equivalent of GNOMIC UTTERANCES and say sad things about Dying or threatening things about regretting it should you try to barge inside. These simply set the mood. The other third will contain valuable KNOWLEDGE or MAGIC formulae for entering. Again, your Tour Mentor will know.

3. In GRIMOIRES and SCROLLS. These always stand out in some way, often by being in another language, but again only about one-third will contain Knowledge. The rest will be threats or sad remarks by copyists.

**INSECTS** are almost nonexistent, possibly as a result of the WIZARDS' WAR (see also ECOLOGY). Parasitic insects such as LICE and bedbugs have mostly been stamped out—although fleas are still popular—and only HOVELS occasionally manifest houseflies. Small numbers of bees must exist, since honey is often served by friendly WIZARDS and people who live in CLIFF DWELLINGS, and so must silkworms, because so many persons wear silken garments. Otherwise, almost the only recorded Insects are the mosquitoes all Tourists complain of in the MARSHES (*in stinging clouds* OMT).

**INVISIBILITY** can be induced by RINGS, CLOAKS, and

MAGIC headgear, and also by competent MAGIC USERS either on themselves or a third party. It seldom occurs to more than one person at once. In essence, Invisibility inhabits that dubious ground between ILLUSION and true Magic. In its minor forms it is a SPELL that says "Don't notice me," which directs the eye of the beholder away from the operator, who is not really Invisible at all. Most Tourists can avail themselves of this Spell when escaping from a CITY. Median forms of Invisibility will make the operator's body wholly transpicuous, but that body will cast a shadow and appear in any MIRROR. Avoid bright lights and reflecting surfaces in these cases, where the Invisibility is really an Illusion. True Invisibility renders the body and its shadow unseeable. This is the rarest and most magical kind. Tourists should bear in mind that all cases of Invisibility are Spells of sight only, and do not affect sounds, SMELLS, and touch. The City GUARD will be able to hear you, smell you, and feel you. Tiptoe past, and do not cough, bump into anyone, or sweat too much.

**INVISIBLE COLLEGE** is used for training WIZARDS and usually occupies a prime site in some major CITY. Once you have penetrated its invisible exterior, you will find it has the usual features of an Oxbridge college—dining hall, buttery, library, towers, lecture rooms, tutors, and even students—but all a little skewed. The Rule here is that, if something magical could possibly go wrong, it will. Be prepared for the Universe to split and for coloured explosions, levitating towers, and tutors in ANIMAL form.

See also APPRENTICES, CITY OF WIZARDS, and HIDDEN CITY.

**IRON** is around in great quantities (this often causes distress to various magical beings), but it is impossible to get to see iron being mined or smelted. The Management doubtless knows why this should be, but Tourists and AVERAGE FOLK are left to conclude that it is All Very Magical.

 **ISLANDERS** are always unusual in some way; this is the Rule. It comes of being descended mostly from PIRATES. At the very least, they are likely to know MAGIC that is not like any other. They tend to build unusually constructed harbours, often defended by Magic. Their SHIPS trade from here. Most Islanders have a strong commercial bent, but under attack they always run about uselessly, and when tidal waves threaten their ISLANDS they have no idea what to do.

 **ISLANDS** are moved about by the Management at will. Sometimes they are in the INLAND SEA, in which case one or more may be the abode of a reclusive WIZARD, and sometimes they are strategically placed at the centre of several sea routes, in which case they are usually the seat of a HIGH KING. Islands further out to sea are traditionally at risk from huge tidal waves generated by underwater volcanoes.
See also ISLANDERS.

*Just when you think the taxes are all paid and there is nothing more to worry about is the time you should leave home secretly. This is just the time when everyone will ask you for money.*

**Ka'a Orto'o**, Gnomic Utterances, *XIV clvi*

**JEWELLERY.** The Rule is that it all has magical purpose. The Management takes the very reasonable line that no one is going to wear or carry something just because it is pretty or beautifully made. Your pendant will always be an AMULET, your brooch a TALISMAN, and your necklace will be of CRYSTAL, which will enable you to communicate with distant friends. If you pick up a piece of Jewellery by the roadside or in a MARKET it will, whatever it looks like, turn out to have some MAGIC. Take care, however. By far the majority of Jewellery is EVIL or, if not Evil, will have conditions attached to its use. For instance, a Ring can either put you under the influence of the DARK LORD or grant wishes while ageing you ten years for every wish. In Fantasyland, even Jewellery you have owned for years will turn out to be something of this kind. If you are lucky, your mother's Ring will merely bring out your latent TALENT. But don't bank on it. Be careful particularly of Jewellery pressed upon you by a dying stranger.

See also JEWELS.

**JEWELS** can, provided they are large enough, be QUEST OBJECTS. Huge rubies, massive sapphires, enormous emeralds, and other great big gems unknown in our world can all be imbued with potencies of various kinds, lost, and then Quested for. Diamonds, oddly, are not much desired, but the rest are eminently collectible. Their exact powers are at the discretion of the Management. Just a few of them have sentimental value only.

See also JEWELLERY.

**JOKES** are against the Rules, except for very bad cumbersome jokes cracked by GUARDS, MERCENARIES, OTHER PEOPLES, and servitors. (It is believed that the Management in fact thinks these are very good jokes, and treasures them.) Everyone else must be deadly serious, although the SMALL MAN, some WIZARDS, and most bad KINGS are allowed to have a sense of humor—and see also THIEVES' GUILD.

**JOURNEY** is of course your Tour. No discovery or action can take place in Fantasyland without a good deal of travelling about. This is in the Rules. The Tour will be set up so that you will find at the outset you need to go to a CITY on the other side of the continent. Once there, you will find you need to go to the extreme south. And so on. You can count on the worst conditions for doing so. (See HARDSHIP, which the Management seems to find synonymous.) (See also LANDSCAPE, ROADS, and TERRAIN, of which you will see lots.) (Oh, and HORSES, which you will have to ride, BOOTS, which you will need when all your Horses are dead, and DARK LORD, who will be trying to stop you every mile of your Journey.)

**JOURNEY CAKE.** See FOOD and WAYBREAD.

**JUGGLERS** are normally hired as extras by the Management and will exhibit their skills in most MARKETS and often also in PALACES. They will be there purely for local colour and your entertainment. In rare cases, the Tourist will need to hide in a troupe of Jugglers and even learn juggling skills. You can tell when you are going to have to do this because the Jugglers will have NAMES.

**JUSTICE** does not exist as such. In some CITIES there will be officials called Justices, but the name means nothing. You will have to pay them and they will then sell you a favourable verdict. Do not look for Justice even in the Court of a GOOD KING. With the best of intentions, the King will be forced to judge against you and may even order you horribly executed. It is better to steer clear of legal matters entirely.

*Kinship is a bondage dragons feel more keenly than men. Their mothers-in-law live longer.*

*Ka'a Orto'o,*
**Gnomic Utterances,** *I iii*

**KING'S MEN** are the elite soldiers who surround any KING. You will encounter three sorts:

1. GOOD. These usually guard a Good King, but on rare occasions you will find them guarding a King that nobody knows is bad. They are very smart and well trained and their drill is as crisp as any you will see. But they are human. At some point you will encounter them in a relaxed mood, joshing their captain, swearing merrily, and recounting touching anecdotes about their young children. They are the salt of the earth, like their King, but there will probably be a time when they have to arrest you. When this happens, they will tell you how much they regret it and not give you any chance to escape. You will have to rely on outside help for that.

2. BAD. These guard either a bad King or a feeble one. Outwardly they seem like the GOOD guards, but in reality they are cruel and coarse. You can tell they are because they swear nastily and their quarters are a mess. When

these arrest you, they will find every opportunity to kick you or twist your arm. They will lick their lips when they hear you are to be put to the TORTURE and ask to watch.

3. Automata. These are always in full ARMOUR and HELMETS (with the visors down). This is because they are not human anymore. The DARK LORD has made their wills his own, and they behave as if they are clockwork, often in unison. They keep coming at you while you are killing them. Usually these GUARDS are in the employ of a puppet King or a MINION OF THE DARK LORD, but sometimes there are whole ARMIES of them directly under the command of the Dark Lord. It is hard to see why the Dark Lord goes to the trouble of enslaving so many minds, unless the aim is to produce ideal soldiers, in which case a good Sergeant Major is probably cheaper and quicker.

**KINGS** come in four kinds:

1. Puppet Kings. These are EVIL, entirely under the power of the DARK LORD, usually through the use of some magic-psychic device such as a glowing RING or a CRYSTAL BALL. You can detect them by the empty look in their eyes and by the fact that their followers behave like automata (see KING'S MEN). They will be very dangerous and must be either tricked or released from their bondage to the device.

2. Bad Kings. These manage to be EVIL entirely on their own. They are harder to detect, because they often have the air of quite pleasant people and, indeed, usually have some good traits of character, such as strength of mind and intelligence. The main way of discovering they are bad is to see how polite they are. Truly Evil Kings are very polite. They will offer you all sorts of luxuries and attempt to divert you from the Tour by every courteous ploy they

can think of. Only when you refuse will they show their true colours, after which they will imprison you.

3. Good Kings are rough diamonds and the salt of the earth. They are easy to detect by their bluff manner and the lack of riches or protocol in their Court. The very best Good Kings always have their crowns on crooked.

4. Long-lost Kings. These are Kings who have been hidden or mislaid soon after birth. They are normally rather young and will be using the Tour to acquire both experience as rulers and various items of Royal regalia (SWORD, SCEPTRE, RING, CUP, etc.) which have been lost at least as long as they have. There is, however, a subsection of long-lost Kings who have been magically deprived of their THRONES. This will have been done either by the implanting of false memories or, in extreme cases, by transplanting the monarch to another body. In these cases the throne will be held by a usurper. Otherwise the same Rules apply. There is obviously a bit of an overlap between long-lost Kings and MISSING HEIRS, but you can generally tell the difference when you see one: a Missing Heir is almost inhumanly naive.

Note that many Kings have a curious relationship with the patch of land they happen to be entitled to rule. If they are absent too long or failing in their duties, crops will not grow, cattle will die, and there will be general bad luck. COUNTRIES where a formerly good King develops a serious personality problem will in sympathy evolve a malign micro-climate, entailing drought in winter, snow in summer, and rain during the harvest. This may be one reason why the choice of FOOD in Fantasyland is so limited.

**KITCHEN.** The place where STEW gets made. In CASTLES, INNS, and PALACES there are always large greasy stone

Kitchens, usually with an open fire where cauldrons of Stew are boiling and the occasional CHICKEN is roasting. Kitchens are presided over by both male and female COOKS, though the Cook in an Inn is regularly female; all have the vilest possible tempers. There will be a lot of shouting and much hurrying about with enormous platters. Helpers in a Kitchen have a miserable time and may often be hit over the head with ladles, etc., for failing to wash dishes quickly enough. Most Tourists will at some time in the Tour get a stint as a Kitchen helper, mostly when MONEY runs out but sometimes as a disguise or because a MAGIC USER has decided to punish them. When this happens, see if the Cook is fat or thin. A glance at her/his COLOUR CODING might be useful too. Some turn out to have hearts of gold under the apron and the shouting. Some are just swine, in which case you can only suffer.

**KNITTING.** It is possible that Knitting has not yet been invented in Fantasyland—at least so far as mortals are concerned (see CRONE). The complete absence of SOCKS and sweaters suggests that the inhabitants have concentrated instead on EMBROIDERY and weaving.

**KNOWLEDGE** can, in rare cases, be your QUEST OBJECT, but only if it is very important, such as the one fact or PROPHECY which will be essential if you are to go about SAVING THE WORLD. Very often, this Knowledge appears in pieces, which the Tourist must collect and assemble in the correct order, and then endeavour to understand before action can be taken. Sometimes there is the added twist that the Knowledge has been collected without your knowing it. In this case, you must have an inspiration before recognising it. A friendly WIZARD or Tour MENTOR can help here. They will madden you, but they will give hints.

K
L

*"Laugh long, live long,"* was the saying of the Sage Grometherus. He took poison to prove it and died chuckling.

*Ka'a Orto'o,*
**Gnomic Utterances, XXXIX i**

**LANDLORDS** are always INNKEEPERS. The term is never used for those who own property for rent.

**LANDSCAPE.** During a Tour, both Tourists and Management will be kept too busy to examine the Landscape much. The Management will draw your attention to a view only when it is likely to prove a threat. Thus a WOOD will be mentioned if the TREES or WOODSMEN are going to be hostile, MOUNTAINS will figure if you are going to have to cross them in bad WEATHER, and steep-sided gorges are delineated when you are about to be AMBUSHED there. If you want to know what the average Landscape is like, consult the cover of any brochure. Here you will see a range of spiky Mountains in the distance, from which a tall WATERFALL descends adorned with a rainbow at its crest. There will be huge and intensely gnarled Trees in the foreground, and both these features will dwarf the line of horsemen making its way across a misty green plain towards the Mountains. The sky is orange and purple. *This* is what Fantasyland really looks like. This is what entices Tourists to enrol for Tours.

**LANGUAGES** are seldom as numerous or as difficult to learn as those of our own world. Most Tours arrange for all inhabitants to speak the same Language or else for most people to know the Common Tongue, even if they speak some other tongue to their families. The exception to this is the OTHER CONTINENT, where the Tourist will have to master a little of the Language. On some Tours, the Management will arrange for a convenient translation SPELL to be cast just as the Tourist is entering the world. But none of this applies to MAGIC. The Language of Spells is usually highly obscure. Sometimes it is the same as the Old Tongue, sometimes not. The Old Tongue is what the really important SCROLLS will be written in (possibly in HIEROGLYPHS or RUNES), and you will need a translator for that. There is only one of it. Evidently the former inhabitants spoke only the one Language. This seems to make it very potent. Just occasionally, when a Tourist is truly beleaguered by Magic, either trying to get through a magic door that will not open or about to lose to someone EVIL, the Old Tongue has a way of suddenly making itself known. Then the Tourist will find her/himself crying out strange words. But do not expect this to happen much.

See also CAPITAL LETTERS and SPEECH.

**LARGE MAN** may not join the Tour until encountered aboard the Slave GALLEY. He is very calm, very strong, and not at all stupid. In some cases he will have been a BLACK-SMITH, which accounts for the ease with which he severs the chains in the Galley. He is often a BARBARY VIKING as well, in which case he will enjoy killing people, preferably more than one at once. In some cases, he is also ELITE, and the Gods take an interest in him; from the moment he joins the Tour, things start to get busy.

**LAST BATTLE.** See CONFRONTATIONS.

**LEATHERY-WINGED AVIANS** usually attack the party early in the Tour, always at night, and generally on an exposed hilltop. You can tell they are about to attack because of the SMELL (see also *REEK OF WRONGNESS* **OMT** and DANGER). They will be beaten off quite easily, but it will be a good scrap. They have probably been sent by a MINION OF THE DARK LORD to feel out the strength of the party, and will not reappear. Since it is always dark when they attack, it is hard to get much idea of their appearance, but they are thought to be about four feet from wingtip to wingtip, with sharp claws and teeth (*razorlike* **OMT**). Where they inflict a wound, that wound will fester instantly. As to their origin, they seem to be some WIZARD's attempt to create pterodactyls (see BREEDING PROGRAMMES and ECOLOGY).

**LEGENDS** are an important source of true information. They always turn out to be far more accurate than HISTORY. Listen and attend carefully if anyone recounts you a Legend. The person telling it may be an old HERBWOMAN, a BARD, a bad KING, one of your COMPANIONS, or just someone in an INN. But no matter how improbable the story, it will always turn out to be the exact truth, and only by following it accurately can you hope to succeed in your QUEST. The Management will never allow anyone to tell you a Legend unless it is going to be important for you to know.

**LICE** seem to be extinct in Fantasyland, possibly because of the good management of the Management. Fleas, by contrast, infest most BLANKETS and all BEGGARS—they are among Fantasyland's very few INSECTS.

**LIGHTING**—unless Magical (see MAGELIGHT and WITCH-LIGHT)—is nearly always primitive and inconvenient, unless magically supplied. There are, in order of frequency:

1. Torches, which are used particularly in PALACES, CASTLES, and DUNGEONS, but also in the streets. These consist of a hefty stick with something flammable at one end. They are not at all convenient, since they are always *flaring* **OMT** and *guttering* **OMT** and must constitute a considerable FIRE risk in TOWNS where buildings are mostly of wood. They frequently blow out (the Rule here is that they do so at the worst possible moment) or simply burn away and plunge you into darkness while you are underground.

2. Candles, either solitary or in candelabra. These are used in INNS and other indoor places. Again there is risk of Fire during TAVERN BRAWLS, but Brawls very seldom do that amount of damage.

3. Rocks deep underground which glow with an eerie light of their own. Fortunately, these are often found moments after your torch has burnt out.

4. Glowbaskets. These are popular in some areas and may be magical. Usually they are a handwoven basket hung high on a wall and filled with something that glows with *a soft greenish light* **OMT**. The contents of the baskets may be either some form of mutant glowworm or stones, possibly chipped from the rocks that glow underground.

5. Lanterns—which, in the absence of electricity, might be supposed to be the most practical form of shielded

light—are surprisingly uncommon and used mostly on the infrequent carriages (see TRANSPORT).

6. SWORDS.

**LITTLE PEOPLE** come in all sizes, from knee-high right up to the shoulder of the average human, and in a variety of breeds. The general Rule is that the smaller kinds are more like humans, while the larger ones get hairier and hairier, beginning with hairy feet and ending with hairy everything. All of them live in secret retired places, in either WOODS or MOUNTAINS, and come out only to join the Tour and help in SAVING THE WORLD. They are surprisingly cheerful, efficient, and brave, and usually win through where humans fail. If you have one or more on your Tour, count yourself lucky. Apart from anything else, Little People are allowed to make JOKES.

**LOST LANDS,** which are like Atlantis or Eldorado in our own world, are surprisingly frequent. Fantasyland seems to have been losing bits of itself for a long time. This happens most often on the PanCeltic TOUR, where the LOST LAND must as a matter of course be visited to acquire items of regalia or QUEST OBJECTS unaccountably mislaid there. There is a strong suggestion always that the LOST LAND is also really the Land of the Dead, in which case Tourists must be careful not to assume that they are dead when they get there, or they might not be able to leave.

**M**

**MAGE.** A fully qualified MAGIC USER who is either in the wings or taking only a cameo role in the action. Bit-part Mages are usually present as a team. The exception to this is the GAY MAGE, who is on his own and a Tour COMPANION.

**MAGELIGHT OR MAGEFIRE** is so common among MAGIC USERS that it is probably what an APPRENTICE Wizard learns to do on his first day. The operator simply thinks, and a small ball of bluish or white light appears either on the hand or hovering in the air, at the shoulder, above the head, or on the end of the STAFF. Magelight has two uses: it gives light in dark places, and it shows that the maker can do MAGIC. When a more powerful Magic User overwhelms the one making the light, the Magelight normally flickers and dims away. Thus it is also a sort of Magic meter. It is otherwise not good for anything much, but it would be nice to be able to do it.

See also WITCHLIGHT.

**MAGIC** has slightly different Rules for every Tour. Tourists had better find out swiftly which Rules apply or there could be problems. Luckily the Management seldom or never changes the Rules in mid-Tour, but it has been known to reserve one or two extra SECRETS for a nasty surprise later on. Even when the Rules are very clear, a Tour will have several different systems of Magic in operation. This is because Magic is an impure art. You will have to contend with at least three of the following kinds:

1. Magic that exists like liquid in a reservoir. Here the operator simply attaches a sort of magical hose and draws off what she/he needs. Attaching the hose often takes a trance to do, whereupon the operator also becomes the hose. HEALERS use this method.

2. Magic that is rather like electricity. Here the process is a longer one. The Magic has first to be generated or acquired by invocation; then it must be shaped or fed into the machinery (this is usually done with diagrams, RUNES, and incantations); and finally it must be plugged in to operate by GESTURE or word of POWER. (See SPELLS.)

3. Mind Magic. This is quicker. The operator simply *concentrates* (OMT). This system applies to FARSEEING, FIRE-STARTING, FORESEEING, MINDSPEECH, TELEKINESIS, TELEPORTING, and most SHAPESHIFTING.

4. Thought Magic. Here the operator can, simply by having very powerful ideas, send out physical feelings that wound, cure, or transform another person. The red-eyed MINIONS OF THE DARK LORD do this when pursuing Tourists. The OMT is *baleful influence*. The afflicted Tourist will feel cold, weak, and contaminated, and may take days to recover. The Rules forbid Good WIZARDS to do this back to the forces of Dark, although they could, quite

M

easily. They have to leave this to a humble Tourist, who will confront the DARK LORD and pour thoughts of GOOD at him. It is very effective. The Dark Lord usually finds this as painful as a bath of acid.

5. Sympathetic Magic. This is when the operator takes a piece of something/someone, such as a wood splinter or a nail clipping. Sometimes this is made into a small model, and named if necessary. The piece is then moved about like a computer mouse and the bigger object/person will do exactly the same, just like the mouse pointer. Many CURSES act this way. You have to repossess the piece. Alternatively, the piece of you that is used is nothing physical, but instead your NAME. Repossessing this can be more difficult.

6. Magic with a price. Here the operator has to pay in some way for the Magic used. This may be selling her/his soul to a DEMON, or simply becoming very tired. Setting WARDS seems to act this latter way.

7. Nature Magic. This often involves HERBS, though it can also be done by attuning to TREES and breezes and things. The operator uses the correct natural object and the result follows.

8. Pattern Magic. Here the Magic lies like threads in a design. The operator perceives this by WITCH SIGHT, takes up the threads, and tugs.

9. MUSIC.

10. Alien Magic. DEMONS, DRAGONS, ELVES, GNOMES, GODDESSES AND GODS, and MARSH DWELLERS all have Magic that works in a quite different way from any of the above. The Rules are not known.

**MAGICIAN.** A MAGIC USER who knows about the mechanics of SPELLS. Get him to check your SWORD.

**MAGIC OBJECTS** can be almost anything, but the important ones are usually QUEST OBJECTS too. There are two kinds:

1. Objects that have been bewitched or bespelled. This can be a temporary SPELL on a BUILDING or a coal scuttle or a BOOT, to make it behave in a startling way; or it can be an enchantment carefully crafted to be permanent. Spells on SWORDS, RINGS, and JEWELS are normally of this kind.
2. Objects that contain their own Magic. This is done by
   A) Making the Object of some substance, such as CRYS-TAL, that gives off Magic like radioactivity. ORBS are like this.
   B) Making the Object in a certain way; for instance, SCEPTRES, STONE CIRCLES, and some SWORDS are Magic because they are the shapes they are. If a Tourist is stupid enough to twist a gem out of a Sceptre or remove a STONE from a henge, or hammer out the rib down the centre of a Sword, none of them will work properly.

**MAGIC USERS.** Anyone capable of using MAGIC. They range from the untaught or APPRENTICE or NOVICE right through to WIZARDS and DARK LORDS. Most have NAMES that describe their status or speciality, such as ENCHANT-RESS, MAGE, Necromancer (see NECROMANCY), but they all have in common the fact that they were born with magical TALENTS/GIFTS. Some never come to very much, but most go on to years of rigorous training and studies. The result nearly always seems to be that their lives get incredibly prolonged. Wizards live for thousands of years. It seems that the longer a person marinades her/himself in Magic, the longer she/he lives. Only HEALERS seem to be exempt from this Rule.

**MAIDS.** These are well built young women (*buxom* **OMT** and *sweating* (OMT)) who wait at table or act as barmaids in the taprooms of all INNS. Traditionally, they are always in a hurry because there are too few of them and too many patrons, all of whom are shouting for service; they are further distracted by the INNKEEPER bawling incomprehensibly at them.

See also BAR SERVICE and EUNUCHS.

**MANAGEMENT** is the body who has arranged this Tour for you. It has made up the Rules for your comfort and convenience, so that no Tourist will ever be taken by surprise or shocked by an unexpected INCIDENT. Management reserves the right to alter the Rules in accordance with current fashions, and will admit absolutely no complaints or responsibility. It wishes you a safe and happy Tour of Fantasyland.

**M**

**MANAGEMENT DIRECTIVES** occur when the Management requires heavenly choirs to add to the usual OFFICIAL MANAGEMENT TERMS (OMTs). This is when the Tour gets particularly *doom laden* (OMT) usually in the lead-up to the CONCLUSION. Then the OMTs go into overdrive and start saying things backwards. Typical MDs are *Grim were they and of awesome countenance*, or *Wan was that dawn and spectral the Sun*, or *High and frowning were the walls but undaunted was the assault thereon*, or *Sang they with eagerness and sang their swords with them*. Anyway, you'll know one when you see one.

**MANSIONS** are rare and usually rather tumbledown BUILDINGS. They are where lords and BARONS live. Their chief features are wall tapestries, oak staircases, an elderly butler, a gallery of family portraits, and GHOSTS. Expect to be uncomfortable in any Mansion. The four-poster BEDS will certainly be damp. However, you will be spared from having to sleep much in yours thanks to haunts, VAMPIRES, and other INCIDENTS.

**MAP.** See Introduction for description. We must emphasize again here that no Tour is complete without a Map. Further, you must not expect to be let off from visiting every damn place shown on it.

**MARKETS** are a feature of every TOWN of any size. They comprise stalls and BOOTHS and lots of SMELLS and shouting. It is where you go for local colour, though you may buy cooked food in insanitary wrappings if you feel so inclined (see SQUALOR). Stalls sell mostly food, Booths clothing, armour, and jewellery. There are also plentiful fresh vegetables on sale. You might as well buy some, as no one else seems to eat the things. This is the place where you will come for your SWORD, CLOTHING, and possibly your HORSE. You will be cheated. If you need a jobbing MAGICIAN to test your Sword (this is strongly advised: see SWORDS), you will find him here in a Booth in one corner.

**MARSH DWELLERS** are the Basques of Fantasyland, entirely different from other PEOPLES and quite as anxious to be independent. They can be human or Other. In either case, they are smallish, brownish, a little twisted (perhaps rheumatically, since they DWELL in such a wet place), with thin limbs and wild brownish weedy hair. They worship an entirely different God, who requires much drumming and lots of SACRIFICES (which involve impaling the victim on a stake), and they use a form of MAGIC that no one else can use. They are expert at lurking entirely unseen until the Tour party is thoroughly lost in the MARSHES, whereupon they will spring out and capture everyone. They will then keep everyone prisoner in a pit, under a net, inside a fence of long thorns, or just unable to move because of Magic, until the ritual hour for Sacrifice has come. Tourists are advised to attempt to persuade these people not to kill them before this hour arrives. This is not easy, since the Marsh Dwellers speak a strange LANGUAGE, but usually an interpreter is provided, almost *but not quite* too late to be of use. After that, there will be apologies and then a feast of ROOTS.

**MARSHES** are an area in the southern-central part of the continent where everything suddenly goes wrong and different. The Management has usually thoughtfully provided you with a BOAT shortly before you enter the Marshes; if not, you should acquire one soonest. The land here becomes mostly WATER, winding sluggishly in multiple channels between banks and islands too soggy to bear your weight. Generally, unpleasant drooping Trees clutch at you as you punt past and brakes of gigantic rushes look *ineffably menacing* (OMT); all this adds to your confusion about which is north and also harbours millions of mosquitoes (*in stinging clouds* (OMT)) which will eat you alive. You will at this stage be lost, foodless, and without WATER. You will not dare to drink from the muddy channels—and with good reason. Strange squirming things swim there, and sometimes there are predators. On some Tours, the overhanging Trees are replaced by small thorny bushes, but the only difference is that the mosquitoes come out at night when you attempt to CAMP on a muddy ISLAND, and by day a cruel wind sweeps over everything. In both cases you will be overwhelmed by *dread* (OMT) and *a sense of danger* (OMT). After a few days of it all, you will almost be glad when the MARSH DWELLERS take you prisoner. They will at least drag you to the only firm ground in the area.

M

**MAYOR.** The head of the TOWN COUNCIL and usually a bumbling idiot. Quite often he is a MINION OF THE DARK LORD, but only a minor one. Keep out of his way.

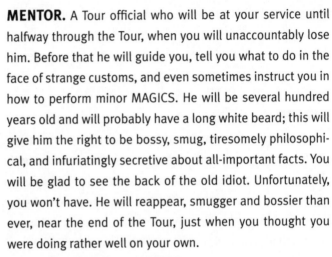

**MENTOR.** A Tour official who will be at your service until halfway through the Tour, when you will unaccountably lose him. Before that he will guide you, tell you what to do in the face of strange customs, and even sometimes instruct you in how to perform minor MAGICS. He will be several hundred years old and will probably have a long white beard; this will give him the right to be bossy, smug, tiresomely philosophical, and infuriatingly secretive about all-important facts. You will be glad to see the back of the old idiot. Unfortunately, you won't have. He will reappear, smugger and bossier than ever, near the end of the Tour, just when you thought you were doing rather well on your own.

See also MYSTICAL MASTERS.

**MERCENARIES** are soldiers for hire who fight WARS they are not really interested in for (a) pay and (b) the raping and looting they get when a CITY falls. Their aim is to survive to enjoy this part, so they are mostly very good soldiers indeed, although they are sometimes rather rough-and-ready-looking in their CLOTHING. Either male or female (see FEMALE MERCENARY), they are drawn, it is stated, from all over the continent, but when you get down to enquiring you find that most of them come from places that are hardly on the MAP—unless they are female captains, in which case they are from a distant NUNNERY. Their leader is always male and mostly has the total loyalty of all these rough types. And they are very well organized. They spend the summers in paid fighting and retire to winter quarters until the fighting starts again in the spring. Here even the

M

roughest types will carve exquisite statuettes in the long winter evenings after they have finished the day's training. Some even read books. The people who employ Mercenaries are normally the more corrupt of the MERCHANT FEUDALISTS, until there is War throughout the land. Then the Mercenaries join the rest of the forces of GOOD. Do not be put off by all the drinking and fighting Mercenaries do. They are going to be on your side in the end.

**MERCHANT FEUDALISTS** are organized in clusters of little COUNTRIES, mostly along the coast, each ruled by a COUNCIL. These trade with one another and are among the few PEOPLES who seem to trade overseas as well. Spices, silks, and olives are mentioned by the Management here. There is no unity among Merchant Feudalists. They all want to see their neighbours dead or reduced to penury. By the judicious use of POISON and MERCENARIES, they often do.

**MERCHANTS**—when freelance—travel from an unknown place in the south northwards to another uncertain place. They own CARAVANS loaded with BALES. And they love MONEY. This must be the reason so many of them travel, because nearly all of them fall by the wayside, victims of BANDITS or other AMBUSHES, and the rest must know the risk. But they keep coming. Individual Merchants are *portly*(OMT), warmly dressed, and rather prone to trust hired GUARDS on small evidence. While alive, they drive a hard bargain. Many of them travel with young female relatives. This is unwise. See SLAVES, FEMALE.

**MINDSPEECH** is the regular term for Telepathy among MAGIC USERS. Almost everyone with a spark of TALENT is able to do it with both humans and ANIMALS. The Tourist may be disconcerted at first when a voice speaks out of nowhere soundlessly inside her/his head, but it will shortly come to seem quite natural. And do not be alarmed in case the Mindspeaker might be able to read your inmost thoughts: usually this is not so, or, if it could be done, the Magic User has sworn not to. Only the DARK LORD breaks this Rule: he will meanly try to read your weaknesses and worst fears and use them against you.

**MINES** are strategically placed in most hills of any stature that are some distance from anywhere civilized. They are of two kinds:

1. Made by DWARFS. The Rule here is that the Mine is either long deserted or at most is inhabited by a few survivors who will make confused claims to have been driven out/ decimated by humans/other Dwarfs/MINIONS OF THE DARK LORD. Inhabited or not, this Mine will be very complex, with many levels of galleries, beautifully carved and engineered. What was being mined here is not always evident, but at least some of the time it will appear to have been JEWELS, since it is customary to find unwanted emeralds, etc., still embedded in the rock on the walls. Metal will also be present, but only when made up into armour and weapons (*wondrous* **OMT**).

2. Manmade. This type of Mine appears to exist for punishment only. It is where prisoners of the DARK LORD or recalcitrant male SLAVES are sent to work. The Mine will abound in whip-wielding overseers (*brutal* **OMT**), chains for the inmates, crude ladders and props, and carts to carry the Mine produce *rumbling through the passages* **OMT**. The miners will be working very hard, but just exactly what they are mining is, as with 1, some-

M

thing the Management is very coy about. Since miners die here in droves, it is possible that the substance mined is dangerous. It could be uranium.

**MINIONS OF THE DARK LORD** are all over the place. The DARK LORD has been busy planting them for years. They can be either male or female. All will be carefully supplied with the means to slaughter Tourists appropriate to their station.

1. Males are bad KINGS, puppet Kings, DUKES, POWER-hungry usurpers, most HIGH PRIESTS, ambitious MERCHANT FEUDALISTS, BARONS, COURTIERS, fat PRINCES, Evil WIZARDS, REGENTS, all ENEMY SPIES, and anyone who suddenly conquers a CITY just as the Tour arrives. We must add to this GOBLINS, TROLLS, and random Other PEOPLES.
2. Females are ENCHANTRESSES, Evil WITCHES, some HIGH PRIESTESSES, and most bad QUEENS.

It will be seen that the Dark Lord prefers to employ males; they seem to respond better to his *wiles*(OMT), especially if they are in a position of power. But he has other shots in his locker, such as:

3. EUNUCHS, MUTANT NASTIES, and carefully selected MONSTERS.
4. UNDEAD or Demonic persons, most of them red-eyed, wearing black and *riding black steeds*(OMT). These persons always have formidable MAGIC and usually operate by night. By day, they rely on brain-dead human soldiery (such as bad KING'S MEN) to keep up the pursuit.

**MINSTREL** used to be a grand term, equivalent to BARD or Harper. These days it mostly refers to the humbler form of musician who plays busily (and probably hungrily) in a gallery all through a feast.

See also MUSIC.

**MIRRORS** are somewhat infrequent, despite the fact that glass is used for windows. Many of them are made of polished metal and are the property of rich people or ENCHANTRESSES. Do not expect to find one in any INN. Where mirrors exist, of whatever material, they are not commonly used for combing the hair in. They will be employed for PROPHECY or FARSEEING or, less frequently, as the way in from our own world to start the Tour, or simply for travel. Glass mirrors are almost exclusively used as a device for spotting VAMPIRES or other ENEMIES in disguise.

**MISSING HEIRS** occur with great frequency. At any given time, half the COUNTRIES in Fantasyland will have mislaid their Crown PRINCESS/PRINCE, but the Rule is that only one Missing Heir can join your Tour at a time. Yours will join as a COMPANION selected from among the CHILD, the TALENTED GIRL, or the TEENAGE BOY, and as part of your QUEST you will have to get them back to the Kingdom where they belong. This can be a right nuisance. All Missing Heirs shine with innocence (some of them quite dazzlingly), and most have very little brain, which means that they will not pick up *any* hints as to their true status. You have to do this for them. In addition, they all have a lot of inborn Royal Qualities such as chivalry, extreme (and embarrassing) honesty, a tendency to give away everything to BEGGARS, and a natural desire for the best of everything for everyone. Since they usually have at least one untrained Royal TALENT too, they can be quite a handful. When the ORB, SCEPTRE, SWORD, etc., start accepting them, this usually makes things worse. But do not despair. Their characters improve at once as soon as they get back where they belong.

Heirs go missing for a variety of reasons:

1. The THRONE was usurped and the False Monarch or-

M

dered the Heir killed. Faithful servitors hid her/him with a poor family instead. See BLACKSMITH.

2. The previous Royal Heir secretly married an unsuitable girl, who fled with her child back to her family. See BLACKSMITH again.

3. A GODDESS OR GOD, for inscrutable reasons, removed and hid the Heir.

4. A WIZARD, for equally inscrutable reasons, did the same.

5. The Royal Family has for centuries been obliged to hide from the DARK LORD, who killed all the previous generation before the latest Heir could be told of her/his BIRTHRIGHT.

6. All the Royal Family has died out except for the most distant branch, which consists only of the Missing Heir, living in poverty and ignorance of her/his BIRTHRIGHT. See BLACKSMITH yet again, plus KING, QUEEN, and QUEST.

**MIST** is almost never due to natural causes. It is usually one of the following:

1. WEATHER Control (see STORM CONTROL).

    A) At sea, when it will have been made by a WIZARD, either to cover the approach of PIRATES or to cover your escape from Pirates.

    B) On land, when it is always a bad sign. It will have been made by an Evil MAGIC USER in a ravine to cover an AMBUSH. In open country, it conceals the approach of a hostile ARMY.

2. The *exudations* OMT of ancient EVIL. These creep out like a *miasma* OMT from places where the BLACK ARTS have once been performed. This can date either from the WIZARDS' WAR or from the BEGINNING, when it will have

been made by mistake by some God. It may also hang over the OLD RUINED CITY as a sign that the erstwhile inhabitants were not a good thing.

3. Lumps of loose MAGIC. This kind of Mist can be various colours, the most favoured being red and green (see COLOUR CODING). It comes rolling in of its own accord and, when it engulfs the Tour, you will find all sorts of peculiar things happening. Its usual trick is to give you a vision of some unhappy event in your childhood, but it can cast any kind of ILLUSION the Management wishes.

4. A sign of any Magic being worked. You will find a Wizard making GESTURES, and the result will be first a Mist, followed quite soon by the magical effect desired. For instance, *the mists rolled aside to reveal a doorway in the cliff* (OMT).

5. A sign that there is a PORTAL to some other world. If a MIRROR dissolves into Mist, you can be sure that you will have to go through it.

6. A sign that you have accidentally strayed into a PanCeltic TOUR.

**MONASTERIES.** Thick stone buildings on a steep hill. They are full of passages, cloisters, and tiny cells, all with no HEATING, and inhabited by MONKS, mostly elderly and austere, some rather addled in their wits. At the Monastery's head will be an Abbot, who is often portly and sly. These establishments have three uses:

1. For SCROLLS (see also TEMPLES). Any Scroll containing information vital to the Tour QUEST is likely to be jealously guarded in a Monastery. It is not advisable to say that you have come to look at this Scroll. If the abbot is really sly, he will find two dozen ways of putting you off. You will probably have to steal the Scroll. In

cases where the Monks are willing to let you consult their Scroll, you will find that the keeper of Scrolls has recently lost his reason and the Scroll with it. You will have to search through the disordered (*smelling mustily of old books* OMT and *filled with the plangent scent of ancient minds* OMT) library by night.

2. For sanctuary and rest. In this case, you will come pounding up to the Monastery at dusk, with the forces of Dark hard on your heels. You will have to hammer at the huge (*oaken* OMT) door a lot, but they will let you in. Once inside, you are safe. This kind of Monastery has religious WARDS that really work. But the problem comes when you have to get out again (see SECRET PASSAGES and UNDERGROUND PASSAGES).

3. For sacking. Here you come pounding up to the building with the forces of Dark half a day behind, only to find it a heap of smoking stones. But there will be one survivor (see NUNNERY for the rest of the Rule).

**MONEY.** There is always a question as to how a Tourist acquires Money. The Management does not permit one to bring gold or travellers' cheques on a Tour. Usually a Tourist arrives with just enough to buy equipment, but if not, the Rule is that you must hire yourself on as a CARAVAN GUARD or some other kind of menial (see KITCHEN). Later in the Tour you may have to hire out likewise as a sparring partner at a SCHOOL OF WEAPONRY. Any other funds must be supplied by discovering TREASURE or by theft; note that, whenever you need them, there will be a plentiful supply of EVIL (or at least degenerate) people and/or fat MERCHANTS from whom you can steal with a blithe conscience.

**MONKS** inhabit MONASTERIES and are mostly extras hired

by the Management. Those with NAMES are likely to be either MENTORS or, very rarely, Tour COMPANIONS. Treat all Monks courteously, however. Many of them have KNOWLEDGE you will be glad to hear.

**MONSTERS** are likely to live in WASTE AREAS, CAVES, and OLD RUINED CITIES. You can usually detect their presence by SMELL (see also DANGER and *REEK OF WRONG-NESS*(OMT)). Most of them have something snaky about them. All have prodigious jaws and teeth and tend to drool. They are normally rather large and prone to attacking Tourists around or after twilight. The most dangerous kind are those who have MAGIC or the ability to live half the time in some spirit world. This makes them difficult to kill. The usual practise is to disable the Monster if possible and then run.

See also LEATHERY-WINGED AVIANS and SCALY FOLK.

**MOON(S).** There is usually only one moon visible, as in our own world. This has given rise to the theory that Fantasyland is an Earth-Alternate, but that may be a false idea since there have been rare sightings of other moons in the sky, often two or three at once and in some cases pink or red or blue. One hesitates to query these sightings. Sometimes a cluster of moons hangs forever in the same position in the sky, revealing that Astronomy is not the Management's strong point.

**MOUNTAIN PASS, BLOCKED.** The Rule is that any time you need to get from one side of the MOUNTAINS to the other, the pass across is blocked. The pass will be a narrow rift high in the Mountains, and by the time you have climbed up there, either with the forces of the DARK LORD hard behind you, or knowing you have only so long to get to the other side before the forces of Darkness get there first, you will find the pass . . . impassable. Usually the Management applies this Rule by prudently sending you off in winter, so that the pass is snowbound; on occasion, though, the blockage can be a landslide or a fall of rocks. In some cases, you can go down and round the long way, but mostly you just have to bash on through. Somehow.

See also HARDSHIP and HYPOTHERMIA.

**MOUNTAINS** are always high and mostly snow-capped. There seems to have been no ice age in Fantasyland, so the Mountains rise tens of thousands of feet into pointed, *jagged peaks*(OMT), which have evidently never suffered erosion. They are full of *rocky defiles*(OMT) and paths so steep you have to dismount and lead the HORSES. Almost certainly there will be at some stage a ledge along a cliff that is only a few feet wide with an immense drop the other side. This will be covered with ice. Snow will be sweeping across it. The Rule is that you are always in a hurry at this stage.

**MOUNTAIN TRIBES.** See DWARFS, EYRIE CLANS, GNOMES, GOBLINS, and STRANGE RACES.

**MULES** are the sterile and sexless offspring of a HORSE and a DONKEY and are sometimes used as pack animals on the Tour. The Management, however, is confused as to the nature of Mules and will often refer to them blithely as *mares*. This is probably because Horses in Fantasyland breed by pollination. (See HORSES for a fuller exposition of this important theory.)

**MUSIC** is very important, always GOOD and probably MAGIC, especially if played on a HARP. It seems that DARK LORDS are tone-deaf. They have never been known to employ Music as a WEAPON, or to strike fear and desolation into anyone by means of a bespelled tune. The utmost they ever rise to is chanting in TEMPLES. This is lucky because, on the side of Good, Music has enormous power. It can amplify SPELLS, summon supernatural help, and inspire superhuman courage. On some Tours it is the only vehicle for GOOD Magic.

See also ELVES, PanCelts, and SONG.

**MUTANT NASTIES.** These, as opposed to MONSTERS, are monstrous beings created by some form of evil Wizardry. They can be magically enlarged and blended ANIMALS, or humans reduced to bestial form. It is standard practice for a WIZARD who is setting out to rule the world to surround himself with monstrous mutant helpers as a first step. Other Mutants are left over from the demise of earlier Wizards.

See also BREEDING PROGRAMMES and LEATHERY-WINGED AVIANS.

**MYSTICAL MASTERS.** Your Tour MENTOR is likely to be one of these, on special assignment. Mystical Masters, male, female, and (possibly) neuter or something else, all wear long white ROBES and operate on the side of GOOD. One or more of these will appear to all Tours from time to time in order to give instructions. These instructions will be so obscure that they will be impossible to follow until too late, but afterwards you will feel good that you knew all along.

*Narope, daughter of the Moon Queen of Semirond, bathed daily in the milk of fifty camels. She then applied two magnums of rose-water to counteract the smell. Her mother soon tired of the expense all this entailed and sold her to a nomad when she was fifteen. No one minded, Narope least of all. Despite the milk of camels, she might never otherwise have found a husband.*

*Hag'git'ta onch'a Beggiz*, Anecdotes, *CLI iii**

*The Management gives no reason or apology for deserting Ka'a Orto'o here.

**NAMES** are very potent in Fantasyland. People with no Names always get killed (unless they are powerfully EVIL and have a Name That Must Not Be Spoken, in which case they get killed anyway, but a lot later). Of those who have Names, almost nobody tells anyone else what their Name *really* is, for fear of its being used in a SPELL to enslave them. MAGIC USERS have to be particularly careful of this. But MERCENARIES also tend to call themselves things like Bald Eagle and Silversword, presumably for the same reason (or maybe because their true Names are Joe Coward and Jill Doe). MISSING HEIRS are always called Names like Triggs and Dumpling: when they find their Names are really Prince Tornalorn or Princess Diore, they stop being Missing. This shows how important Names can be. AVERAGE FOLK, SAGES, and some Tourists, however, adopt the expedient of cutting out half their Names and filling the gaps with APOSTROPHES, as in Ka'a Orto'o. Then, unless you know what was in the gap, you can't enslave them. This is the true reason why so many Names in Fantasyland contain Apostrophes.

Many folk—ELVES and DEMONS particularly—are given hugely long Names so that they can be conveniently shortened in this way. Demons, indeed, would have a bad time otherwise. As soon as a Magic User learns a Demon's Name, that Demon has to do anything the Magic User wants.

On some Tours the same prudent coyness applies to MAGIC OBJECTS. The exceptions are SWORDS, who seem very proud of being known to be really Excalibur or Widowmaker.

**NECROMANCY** is, in Fantasyland, the art of raising the dead, and you need a specialized MAGIC USER to do it. You must expect to need to consult someone who is dead about two-thirds of the way through your Tour. You must hire or call in a favour from a Necromancer, who will do things with little pots of smoke over the grave and then summon the dead person in words that vibrate the earth and the air. After this, a misty version of the corpse (or sometimes one not misty enough for comfort) will arise, bringing with it a cold blast of air and a strong graveyard SMELL. This simulacrum will be able to speak and will have all the memories of the dead person. You must ask it what you want to know. But take care to ask the right questions. Usually such a rite cannot be repeated, and the dead are often as literal-minded as computers.

See also BLACK ARTS.

**NOMADS.** See DESERT NOMADS and NOMAD TENTS.

**NOMAD TENTS** have peculiar acoustics, possibly because they are usually constructed of skins over a framework of wood. Perhaps this makes them more like houses. Be that as it may, you will find that you can hold a secret and private conversation in one of these tents without any danger whatsoever of anyone overhearing you. The TENTS of MERCENARY captains and KINGS often display the same properties. Like so many of the marvels of Fantasyland, the secret of these soundproof tents has not yet been imparted to this world.

**NORTHERN BARBARIANS** DWELL in the snowy part behind the northern MOUNTAIN range. They are very barbarous and tend to kill strangers on sight. This is because the males spend their time in longhouses honing their fighting kills. It is not certain what their females do. Northern Barbarians do not feel the cold. They wear only a fur loincloth and copper wristguards. Their real clothing is their WEAPONS. But they are not *stupid* savages, only savages. They use skis and sledges for getting about in the snow and this, given the state of TRANSPORT generally, must be the equivalent of having invented the wheel. When Tourists visit here, they are advised to defeat all Barbarians who attack them. Then the Barbarians will respect them: it is the only Language they understand. The Tourists must then go on to prove the SHAMAN a fraud. After this, a Chieftain will offer the Tour anything it needs.

See also BARBARIAN HORDES.

**NOVICE** is a term in frequent use. There are not only Novice PRIESTS and Priestesses and Nuns: you will also encounter Novice HEALERS and Novice BARDS, and sometimes also Novice MAGES. This reflects the religious awe in which all these callings are held in Fantasyland. Novices are always young, frequently skinny and undernourished, and clad in ROBES (*skimpy* OMT) appropriate to the calling they are learning. Most of them behave as if they have either taken vows of chastity and silence or are very stupid. They do little but agree with the Priest/Bard/Mage to whom they are assigned, and they are utterly loyal to this person. If a Novice behaves in any other way, suspect her/him either of having been got at by the forces of EVIL or of being in fact an APPRENTICE who might at any moment do something foolish with a SPELL. Alternatively, she/he might be a MISSING HEIR.

**NUNNERIES.** The Rule is that any Nunnery you approach, particularly if you are in dire need of rest, Healing, or provisions, will prove to have been recently sacked. You will find the place a smoking ruin littered with corpses. You will be shocked and wonder who could have done this thing. Your natural curiosity will shortly be satisfied, because there is a further Rule that there will be one survivor, either a very young NOVICE or a very old nun, who will give you a graphic account of the raping and burning and the names of the perpetrators. If old, she will then die, thus saving you from having to take her along and feed her from your dwindling provisions; if a Novice, she will either die likewise or prove to be not as nunnish as you at first thought, in which case you may be glad to have her along.

*Onions much attracted the Sage Algeron, who used to declare that onions were like the eyes of demons. Some say it was a demon who took off his left big toe.*

Ka'a Orto'o,
**Gnomic Utterances,** *CCCIX xv*

**OFFICIAL MANAGEMENT TERM** (OMT) appears in this Guide where necessary and in italics. OMTs are forms of words which the Management has dreamed up for use every time a certain thing, fact, sensation, or person is mentioned. Thus STEW is *thick*(OMT) and *savoury*(OMT); HISTORY is *lost*(OMT); at the point where the party of Tourists is about to be attacked *the very air seemed doom-laden*(OMT); and a constant COMPANION on the Tour will be *the rat-faced little man*(OMT). OMTs perform the same function as music in films.

**OFFSHORE ISLANDS** exist in some quantity, some having human inhabitants, and one at least being the abode of DRAGONS. Unfortunately, the only ways to reach these islands are somewhat hazardous for Tourists:

1. If male, you must be captured by PIRATES and sold as a GALLEY SLAVE. You may then row to the vicinity of an island, saw through your chains, kill your owners, and swim

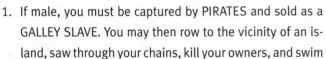

there. (Note that this is impracticable for female Tourists, as female SLAVES are reserved for Another Fate.)

2. If female, you must befriend a Dragon and get flown to the Isle of Dragons.

Yes, it is clear that only males get to visit the human islands and only females find their way to the Dragons. This is the tough, sexist way the Management wrote the Rules.

**OLD RUINED CITY** can be in a WOOD, in the DESERT in a dry ravine, or hidden in the MOUNTAINS. It can be an ANCIENT ENGINEERING PROJECT or just RUINS. You will do quite a lot of Travelling looking for it if you want it as a QUEST OBJECT. Otherwise your Tour will stumble upon it by accident. Either way, it is *beset with Dangers* **OMT**. It will be full of residual MAGIC of an antique and unpleasant kind. The former inhabitants will have set up traps and magical burglar alarms which are still in place after many centuries. These will be nastiest and most active near the TOMB or TEMPLE. Some of the party will have to deactivate these while fighting off hostile tribes, and the rest must go after the SECRET behind the ALTAR.

**OLD TONGUE.** See LANGUAGES.

**OMENS.** See PROPHECY.

**ORBS** are strange things with a double purpose. On one hand they are part of a KING's regalia; on the other they are *numinous* **OMT** objects with minds of their own. In appearance, they are a large ball, the size to fit the hand of an adult male, and they are often made of some very obscure CRYSTAL. This lights up, gives orders, attacks enemies, and communicates with other Kings and the DARK LORD. If they are your QUEST OBJECT they will play hard to get, but end up, almost with a sigh, beaming with coloured light in the hand of the true heir. You feel the Orb has been having fun hiding. So wilful are Orbs that it seems likely that they are in reality the positronic brains of dismembered robots, imported from the SF Tour.

**ORCS** are a newer and better mutation of GOBLINS, even nastier, and always in the service of the DARK LORD.

**OTHER CONTINENT.** This is the second major landmass. It is sometimes brought into play on the Tour, but only if the MAP shows it as fairly close to the continent where the Tour began. Things there are generally much the same as on the first continent but described as *exotic*(OMT), as are its inhabitants, the OTHER CONTINENTALISTS. Probably the main difference will be the FOOD (*highly spiced*(OMT)). You may expect at least one CONFRONTATION there, normally with a female in rather scanty CLOTHING.

**OTHER CONTINENTALISTS** live (*dwell*(OMT)) on the OTHER CONTINENT. They are seldom dissimilar from PEOPLES on the first continent except that, for some reason, they are always members of CLANS. This is so even when the inhabitants evidently belong to the FANATIC CALIPHATES, which they often do, and wear turbans and eat spiced food. This means there is always likely to be a blood-feud and Clan WAR, during which the Tourist must keep her/his head down and try to arrange a passage back to the first landmass, which is normally not difficult. Otherwise, Other Continentalists are mild, reasonable people, although some Tours find they have more than their fair share of seductive older women. In rare cases, the People here are savage xenophobes (see XENOPHOBIA), in which case the Management will get you out of there, quick.

**OTHER PEOPLES.** See PEOPLES and STRANGE RACES.

**OUTER OCEAN.** This is on the MAP, but it is out of bounds for the Tour. You can see that it is from the little drawings all over it. The Management does not know what, if anything, lies beyond this Ocean, and the Cartographer felt free to doodle in the space.

*Politics is when you sell your daughter to bandits and your daughter and your-self are then both set free.*

Ka'a Orto'o,
Gnomic Utterances, *XXXI ii*

**PALACES** are where all rulers and some DUKES live. The Rule is that all Palaces are large and ornate inside, and reached by a triumphal avenue and a long flight of steps. Otherwise they can be of any architectural style. The Management will stop you as you reach the Palace and force you to look at the rows of windows/columns/statues/gilded carvings/domes/fretted towers/lacy spires, and the effect of the gigantic doorways guarded by soldiers. You will have to observe the several wings, courtyards, and gardens. A further Rule seems to be that all this magnificence is of stone, unless it belongs to an ENCHANTRESS or a northerly WIZARD, in which case it will be built of ice. The more normal stone kind has plainly taken many masons and sculptors many moons to make. Sometimes the Management gives you potted HISTORY here, and shows how some parts are old and some newer. Inside, a Palace follows the Rule for BUILDINGS and is even larger, with many long corridors, ballrooms, CHAMBERS, and galleries. Some Palaces are an actual maze in which Tourists may get lost. The THRONE room is usually, but not invariably, the largest and most imposing room of all. There will be paintings, pillars, lackeys, and SLAVES, not to speak of COURTIERS. In more northerly Palaces, banners are hung from high ceilings. There will be at least one INCIDENT in every Palace, usually more. Tourists seldom leave Palaces peacefully by the front entrance.

See also HEATING.

**PanCeltic TOURS** are normally taken separately from the rest of Fantasyland. Here the MAP will be of only one COUNTRY, which has a Welsh name, and shows TOWNS called things like Dun Bhlaioinaidbth (pronounced Dublin) or Glas Uedhaoth (pronounced Glasgow) and rather more MOUNTAINS. The Tour will, however, take place in the usual way, except that PORRIDGE will largely replace STEW and there will be rather more MAGIC. But the WEATHER will be a great deal worse. When it is not raining, everywhere will be hidden (*shrouded*(OMT)) in MIST. If you go on one of these Tours, you will not always find it easy to know either what is going on or what people are talking about. The Mist seems to get into everyone's brains.

**PanCelts** are frequently red-haired. They wear plaids and have NAMES you must consult the glossary in order to pronounce. By the Rules (pronounced GEAS) which govern them, they have to call ELVES Shee (pronounced Sidhe) and refer to the ENEMY as Shadow. Otherwise they are nice people who drink a lot of the water of life (pronounced Uisce) and love to tell you LEGENDS by firelight. They also fight a lot and rather well, since both men and women train hard from the age of ten. But there is no such thing as an ordinary

PanCelt. Each of them is either a MAGIC USER or a BARD or a Druid (pronounced like a sneeze), or sometimes all three (in which case you pronounce it Merlin). They are governed by strong and beautiful QUEENS called things like Maebdh Aeiolaien (pronounced Mad Eileen) or strong and serious KINGS called, for instance, Daibhaeaidhaibh MacAeraith (pronounced Dave Mate), and they appear to worship the Welsh Bard Taliesin. It is in this Bard's honour that they all sing so much, even more than the Shee/Elves do. And, like the Elves, they are prone to go on about how very much better things were in the Old Days, when a HERO could walk in one day from Caer Dibdh to the sea by taking a shortcut through Tir n'an Og (pronounced The Many-Coloured Land).

**PATRONS OF INNS** are mostly AVERAGE FOLK with a sprinkling of STRANGE RACES, and are put in the INN to make the barmaids too busy to serve you and to provide loud conversation shortly followed by a TAVERN BRAWL. In some cases they also show suspicion and *growl* OMT when you talk to them. All of this is known by the Management as "atmosphere." But you should listen to what they say over their tankards of BEER. They will always have the latest rumour, and this will give you a hint about what the DARK LORD is up to now.

P
Q

**PEASANTS.** See AVERAGE FOLK.

**PENTACLE.** See PENTAGRAM.

**PENTAGRAM OR PENTACLE.** Five-pointed figures essential in many forms of ritual MAGIC. It can be drawn both on solid surfaces and in the air. In the latter case, it will *hang there, glowing* OMT.

# WHAT TO PACK FOR YOUR TOUR

Ideally you will want

- *Fleece-lined winter clothing plus tropical garb*
- *Waterproof jacket and leggings*
- *Fleece-lined sleeping bag*
- *Walking boots, riding boots, rubber boots, sandals, trainers*
- *Saucepans, frying pan, jug, plates, cups, water bottle, knife, fork, spoon*
- *A kettle and a teapot*
- *A cauldron for Stew*
- *Tea, coffee, sugar, salt, flour, chocolate in waterproof containers*
- *A large supply of paper handkerchiefs*
- *A thermos flask*
- *An electric torch*
- *A small gas stove*
- *A battery-powered heater*
- *One gross (144) batteries*
- *One mile of nylon rope*
- *Pitons and other climbing gear*
- *At least one gun*
- *Twelve crates of ammunition*
- *At least one very sharp knife*
- *A tent*
- *A hammer*
- *A spade*
- *A sturdy waterproof pack for all this, provided you can lift it*
- *And of course a Sword*

In actual fact, the Management will allow you none of the above. You don't even get to take this Tough Guide. You will go in what you stand up in, with a blanket and a cloak for warmth and only one pair of Boots. You will be allowed to find or purchase your Sword, but forget the rest. As for the paper handkerchiefs, you don't even get a cloth one. If your nose runs, just sniffle or wipe it on your cloak.

**PEOPLES** are of two kinds, human and other:

1. Humans are ANGLO-SAXON COSSACKS, ARISTOCRATIC FEUDALISTS, AVERAGE FOLK, BARBARIAN HORDES, BARBARY VIKINGS, DESERT NOMADS, EYRIE CLANS, the folk of the FANATIC CALIPHATES, ISLANDERS, MERCHANT FEUDALISTS, NORTHERN BARBARIANS, OTHER CONTINENTALISTS, RELIGIOUS FEUDALISTS, TRAVELLING FOLK, denizens of the VESTIGIAL EMPIRE, WAR AND WORSHIP PEOPLE, WARRIOR WOMEN, and WOODSMEN. We should perhaps also include the PanCelts, although they generally have their own Tour. WIZARDS and other MAGIC USERS are mostly thought to be human too, but that was long ago and seems to have worn off. BANDITS, MERCENARIES, PIRATES, and SLAVES are said to be drawn impartially from among the Peoples, but all four types exhibit occasional exotic individuals not easily accounted for. Oh, and Tourists are mostly human too.

2. Other are APELIKE CANNIBALS, ELVES, DWARFS, GIANTS, GNOMES, GOBLINS, LITTLE PEOPLE, MARSH DWELLERS, ORCS, SCALY FOLK, SEA PEOPLES, TROLLS, WERES, and those simply designated STRANGE RACES. Not all of these are friendly to Tourists.

**PERSON.** As a QUEST OBJECT, a Person is very hard to find.  She/he will not be located until two-thirds of the way through the Tour. When found, she/he will be all you expected, but unsatisfactory in some way. If a parent or a WIZARD, she/he will not be able to give the comfort, instruction, or SECRET you needed, and you will spend the rest of the Tour looking for these instead. In rare cases, the Management has you on by having the Person there all along, as a Tour COMPANION. Then the rest of the Tour will be spent helping this Person with the business she/he was on the Tour to perform. See BIRTHRIGHT.

**PIRATES** range the seas in force, though most of them operate individually. When not BARBARY VIKINGS, Pirates are drawn from all populations. The sole qualifications are that they must be rough and ruthless, with a penchant for dressing gaudily. This usually includes pierced ears. The Rule is that Pirates always have the fastest SHIPS, except for Barbary Vikings; so, if the Tour takes you to sea and the lookout reports a Pirate in the offing, expect to be overhauled, grappled, and boarded. Nervous Tourists will be pleased to know that this is a mere INCIDENT, however. Pirates are always beaten off after a bloody swordfight, unless you have not yet been enslaved. Then you will be captured and sold. See GALLEY SLAVE and SLAVE.

P
Q

**PLACE.** If a place is a QUEST OBJECT it is invariably a long way away, Hidden, or obscure. In some cases it can be a small crag designated as a meeting place with persons in urgent need of help. Usually it is a CITY, HIDDEN KINGDOM, ISLAND in a lake, OLD RUINED CITY, STONE CIRCLE, or SECRET VALLEY. In all cases, you will reach it to find the Tour by no means stops here. There will be an interval while you acquire Arcane KNOWLEDGE or SELF-KNOWLEDGE, and then off you will go again to do something about what you learnt.

**PLAGUE** *visits* OMT certain areas unpredictably and kills a lot of people. Though this is not surprising, given the amount of REFUSE lying about, the relative absence of bacteria/viruses suggests that the cause may be magical. Indeed, on investigation, this usually proves to be so. The DARK LORD or a MINION has tried to stamp out a TOWN or CITY. Tourists need not be alarmed. The Dark Lord will not proceed against any Tours with such underhand tricks. No Tourist catches Plague. The normal pattern is for the Plague to have visited ten or so years before your Tour, when it will have killed the parents of at least one of your COMPANIONS. Very rarely, you will enter a City *in the grip* OMT of Plague and be forced to pick your way among hideously blotched (*disfigured* OMT) corpses lying in the streets. But it will not be catching.

**POISON** is in use a lot, primarily by EUNUCHS, MERCHANT FEUDALISTS, and denizens of the VESTIGIAL EMPIRE. Tourists should watch everything they eat or drink around all these kinds of people. They are experts and have Poisons not known in our world. Most Poisons work swiftly, turning the victim a variety of strange colours as they do their stuff; but the most dangerous are the slow Poisons to which only the poisoner has the antidote. You can be enslaved by one of these, because the poisoner will always offer the antidote once a day provided you do what she/he wants. Usually this type of Poison is administered in a drink, but if they hold you down and inject you there is nothing you can do. The Management, fortunately, seldom allows this to happen, possibly because hypodermics are so hard to obtain.

**POLITICS** occur only in the VESTIGIAL EMPIRE and on some PanCeltic TOURS. The Rule is that they are always very complicated and involve issues most Tourists have never heard of. A typical piece of Politics would be:

House/CLAN Frumpus, who worship Ad and trade in leather, have intermarried with House/Clan Trumpus, who worship Bagel and wish for leather concessions in their sheep business, and are allied with House/Clan Dorpus, whose head is a weak person and who trade in perfume and skins and worship Vinus, against Houses/Clans Drumpus, Corpus, and Bremo, who trade in skins, wine, and pottery and worship Bagel, Ord, and Vinus. Because of Bagel- and

Vinus-worship (see RELIGION), Houses/Clans Drumpus, Dorpus, and Trumpus also have a secret understanding against the others. Only one senator can be elected here. While the Houses/Clans manoeuvre, there is also great jockeying for headship inside the Houses/Clans, and people merrily POISON one another. . . .

Anyway, it eventually cancels down to the Head of House/Clan Frumpus, because he is on two sides at once, having to sell himself sheepskins and then Poison himself, leaving the four deities glaring at one another.

**POOLS.** Any Pool is likely to be *numinous* ⟨OMT⟩ or Enchanted. Some give you strange VISIONS when viewed by moonlight, some just give you strange Visions. A few have additional virtues, such as Healing or granting longevity. Some can lead you astray.

The Rule is that, of all prophetic objects (see PROPHECY), only Pools are allowed to give false information—and even they will base their misinformation on true facts. If a Pool is a QUEST OBJECT, it follows the Rule that you have not completed your QUEST by finding it. Often there is something under its surface, such as the transformed body of a Royal heir or a MONSTER, or both, which will give you KNOWLEDGE that requires further action.

**PORRIDGE.** See PanCeltic TOURS.

**PORTALS** can be MIRRORS, Pictures, Standing STONES, STONE CIRCLES, Windows and special gates set up for the purposes. You will travel through them both to distant parts of the continent and to and from our own world. The precise manner of their working is a Management secret.

**POWER** means either ruling a lot of people or very strong MAGIC. In Fantasyland, the two tend to be synonymous.

**PRACTICE RING OR COMBAT RING** is a sanded circle used for sparring and WEAPONS practise; usually it has a paling around it. It can be found attached to any SCHOOL OF WEAPONRY, outside MERCENARIES' winter quarters, and quite often on the outskirts of aggressive TOWNS and VILLAGES. It is always well kept. Fighting is important. Expect at some stage of the Tour to have a practise bout during which your opponent is out to kill or maim you.

**PRIESTS** will be attached to a small local TEMPLE. Some are austere and unpleasant, but most are quite decent people. HIGH PRIESTS are another question altogether.

**PRINCES** are of three kinds:

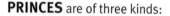

1. Acknowledged heirs to thrones. These Princes are bad lots, fat, greedy, wilful, and cruel at best, usually noted for their *pasty*(OMT) or *puffy*(OMT) faces and their rude, discontented manners. In some way, these will have managed to disguise their natures in front of their Royal fathers the KINGS, who will think the world of them. At their worst, Princes will either be under the thumb of the REGENT, who will have sold his soul/services to the DARK LORD, or the Prince himself will be a MINION OF THE DARK LORD. In this case, there is no nasty sort of cruelty and slyness these Royal heirs will not stoop to. They recognise those of better natures at once and attack them with everything they have.

2. Unacknowledged heirs. These are:
   A) Princes who have been thrown out by their Royal father. These will have been framed by a Chancellor or

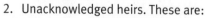

younger Prince (who will be fat, see above) and dis-
inherited for crimes they did not commit.

B) Lost heirs (see MISSING HEIRS), who have been
stolen or removed for safety at their births. These will
not have a notion of who they really are, but will find
out in the course of the Tour.

Both A) and B) are invariably basically GOOD, but hasty,
naive, and with a lot to learn, which the Tour will mostly
teach them. Both will be seeking their BIRTHRIGHTS.

3. Ruling Princes. These rule slightly lesser COUNTRIES and
are normally average to good in their natures. Sometimes they are even better than good Kings, from having
a Princely nature.

**PRINCESSES** come in two main kinds:

1. Wimps.
2. Spirited and wilful. A spirited Princess will be detect-
able by the *scattering of freckles across the bridge of
her somewhat tiptilted nose*(OMT). Spirited Princesses
often disguise themselves as boys and invariably
marry commoners of sterling worth. With surprising
frequency these commoners turn out to be long-lost heirs
to Kingdoms (See PRINCES).

**PRISON** is really a lot of DUNGEONS in one place, plus a
fairly grisly TORTURE Chamber. The prison will be reached
by a stone stair, dampish, lit by torches in brackets on the
walls, and guarded by sadistic soldiery. Most of these
GUARDS are rather careless: they think no one can escape.
All Tours tend to prove this assumption wrong.

See also KING'S MEN.

**PROPHECY** is used by the Management to make sure that

no Tourist is unduly surprised by events, and by GODDESSES AND GODS to make sure that people do as the deity wants. All Prophecies come true. This is a Rule (but see POOLS). The methods used are various:

1. A SEER or MYSTICAL MASTER suddenly gives tongue. This is always unwelcome and usually obscure. The most obscure pronouncements strongly resemble GNOMIC UTTERANCES. A typical example might be: *I see the white eagle flying into the Sun with the red lion in his beak.*

2. Crystal Gazing. This method is without sound and can therefore be misconstrued. See CRYSTAL BALL.

3. DREAMS and VISIONS. These usually give vivid scenes without explanations.

4. Looking into MIRRORS or POOLS/bowls of magically enhanced water or ink. These give limited sights of the future, again without sound but usually in full colour.

5. Casting RUNES or other counters. Here the result must be read by an expert, but it is always very detailed and explicit.

6. Cards, called Tarot by the Management. Here a Fortune Teller will lay out the cards for a reading and explain as it proceeds. A typical layout might go: *Ace of Winds, that's for Talent, and the Wandering Minstrel suggests the Talent is wild; the Queen of Dreams and Knave of Voids are a threat to you; but the King of Castles can withstand it; and here are the Ace and Ten of Jewels in support.* Some packs have up to ten suits, plus wild cards and trumps. Many of them appear to contain only aces and court cards.

7. Omens. These can vary from a sudden blast of wind at a foolish act to a Tour COMPANION becoming suffused with kingly golden light.

8. ASTROLOGY, which is used mostly for large-scale Prophecy to do with SAVING THE WORLD.

# Q

**QUEENS** ruling in their own right are rare, but they do occur. When they do they are:

1. Totally useless because dominated by a male lover or COUNCILLORS, or both.

2. GOOD, but incapacitated by MAGIC or scruples or both. In the most extreme cases, this Queen will sit on her throne perpetually in a state of blanched preservation. Tourists requiring favours of her will need only one look to know that here is something else they have to put right before they can get on with the real business of the Tour. When rescued, such Queens can put things in order with commendable briskness.

3. Good. This Queen will be a MAGIC USER and terribly conscientious. In her case the Tour will reveal something highly amiss with either her COUNTRY or the whole continent. The Queen will often have to join the Tour to put this right (see SAVING THE WORLD). You will have to spend the Tour worrying about the Queen's safety.

4. Old-fashioned bad. This kind of Queen is totally in control. She has everybody terrified of her, possibly through Magic. And, again possibly through Magic, she will be beautiful (see COLOUR CODING, but there is an exception to the usual Rule here: such Queens can be red-haired to show how wilful and bad-tempered they are). Her Country will be the most abject and oppressed of any on the Tour. Since she is very cruel, this will not bother her at all. She will just order in a few more peasant youths to ravish and then dismember. Naturally, she is very sexy. She will demand SEX with most Tourists and one of you will slight her. She will have you put to the TORTURE and then, after you escape, pursue you for the rest of the Tour. The only thing to do is to kill her, but you will not like to strike a woman.

5. A bad mother. This Queen is really ruling for her young son (see CHILDREN), but she will be so anxious to go on ruling that she will be bringing the lad up to be wholly dependent on her. This Queen is a dangerous sentimental bitch, because she will claim that everything she does is for the sake of her Child. She will try to POISON anyone who gets in her way. Only a powerful AMULET will help you here. Naturally no Tourist will want to have anything to do with this Queen, but it will usually be necessary to release the young KING from her clutches before you can proceed on the Tour. The local God may well insist on it.

**QUEST.** Many, possibly most, Tours are organized as a Quest. This is like a large-scale treasure hunt, with clues scattered all over the continent, a few false leads, MYSTICAL MASTERS as game-show hosts, and the DARK LORD and the TERRAIN to make the Quest interestingly difficult. The Management selects a QUEST OBJECT (of which Tourists are normally informed either at their STARTING POINT or no later than six INCIDENTS after), then adds the various INCIDENTS, CONFRONTATIONS and FIGHTS, plus a stew of all the other items you find listed here in *Toughpick*. Places where clues to the Quest Object can be found are listed in the appropriate entries, but Tourists should stay alert both to statements made by, say, dying GOBLINS and to the behaviour of the DARK LORD: much can be learnt from what he does not want you to do. You should then have a thoroughly eventful Tour without ever feeling truly at a loss. The Rule is that Tours will always succeed in a Quest, so the Management will give you hints if you go off in the wrong direction (see PROPHECY). In order to be assured of your future custom, the Management has a further Rule: Tourists, far from being rewarded for achieving their Quest Object, must then go on to conquer the Dark Lord or set about SAVING THE WORLD, or both. And why not? By then you will have had a lot of practise in that sort of thing and, besides, the Quest Object is usually designed to help you do it.

**QUEST, ETERNAL.** See ETERNAL QUEST.

**QUEST OBJECTS** can be various, but are quite strictly defined by the Rules. They are:

1. Material Objects. CUPS, JEWELS, ORBS, RINGS, SCEPTRES, STONES, and SWORDS.
2. Places. HIDDEN KINGDOMS, ISLANDS, OLD RUINED CITIES, POOLS of enchantment, STONES, TEMPLES, VALLEYS, and, less frequently, Fountains (which may double up as Fountains of Youth).
3. PERSONS. See APPRENTICES, HARDSHIP, and PRINCES.
4. KNOWLEDGE. Usually for BIRTHRIGHT or MAGIC or both.
5. Most rarely of all, SELF-KNOWLEDGE.

**QUICKSAND.** This is a hazard that can occur anywhere. Blundering into Quicksand counts as a small INCIDENT; usually there is no BOG handy. Basically, the sandy ground underfoot turns out to be bottomless and everyone starts to sink. Most people make it back to firm ground, but at least one HORSE (*eyes rolling in frenzy* OMT) and one unlucky Tourist will sink and have to be rescued either by the strength of the LARGE MAN or by everyone hauling on ropes.

*Run far and fast when a wizard frowns. If he smiles, run harder. Above all, refrain from laughing when he laughs. But if he weeps, you may join in courteously.*

**Ka'a Orto'o,**
**Gnomic Utterances,** *IX x*

**RABBITS.** Plump furry mammals who live in burrows underground. They have been thoughtfully introduced by the Management as a FOOD source on the Tour. They are quite rare, to judge by the number of times the Management pretends you have caught a Rabbit when you have really caught a HARE, and so may have been introduced only very recently. Rabbits, when they have no natural predators (of which there are none except humans in Fantasyland), always spread uncontrollably and become a pest. This they have evidently not yet had time to do.

**REEK OF WRONGNESS** is the OMT for the sensation you get when you encounter a POOL of EVIL, or when you have been set up for an AMBUSH or BETRAYAL. It is possible that local conditions do give such things a noticeable SMELL.

See also DANGER.

**REFUSE** of a thankfully unspecified kind is obligatory in the streets of TOWNS and CITIES. Sometimes it lies about in such heaps that you will feel it fortunate there are so few germs in Fantasyland. See also ECOLOGY.

**REGENTS.** These are hale men in their early forties, often DUKES, who have charge of a Kingdom while the monarch (usually a KING, but sometimes a QUEEN, here indistinguishable from a spirited PRINCESS) is too young to rule. Nine-tenths of them are EVIL. They have the young ruler under their thumbs in a variety of unpleasant ways, and do not intend to give up ruling even when the monarch comes of age. Most of them plot to kill her/him then. Nearly all of them are bluff, pleasant, and richly dressed, so Tourists may have trouble discerning their true Evil until proof is supplied. Luckily the Management will supply it as soon as the Tour is settled in the PALACE and is just about to go to sleep for the night. The Regent must then be unmasked and the young monarch freed from her/his toils; but this will not be easy. The Regent is up to most tricks and will fight back hard. In some cases, the Regent will not be hale, but sickly and careworn. Be careful of Regents who are like this. They are worse than the healthy kinds.

R

**RELIGION** is varied and widespread. The Rule is that, even among rational peoples, all adherents are extremely devout and in many places worship is fanatical. The exceptions to this Rule are all Other PEOPLES, who do not appear to have Religions; NORTHERN BARBARIANS, who believe only in spirits and themselves; and BARBARY VIKINGS, who believe in nothing. Anywhere else you have to be careful what you say about GODDESSES AND GODS. There are three sorts of Religious beliefs:

1.  One God. This belief is generally represented as the newer

Religion, but only if the one God is masculine. Often, this male God is supposed to be the Sun, but sometimes he just *is*. Even when his worshippers see him as benign, they tend to hate women and MAGIC USERS (especially WITCHES, who are both). At their worst, they become extremely cruel: they make strict and arbitrary laws and stamp out all other beliefs as heresy. They also have a tendency to build a lot of oppressive TEMPLES. If, on the other hand, the one God believed in is female, she will be a GOOD deity and her worshippers nice people. They will worship her out of doors or in small shrines, with singing and very charming festivals. The exceptions here are the WAR AND WORSHIP PEOPLE, whose Goddess is highly puritanical and appears to be an ASPECT of Nature at its worst. This probably reflects the state of the ECOLOGY.

2. Three Gods. This is supposed to be the older, gentler belief. Certainly, those who believe in threesome Gods simply get on quietly with their devotions, not attempting to convert or persecute anyone else. Opinions differ as to the constituents of this Triad. Some Tours give it as being a Mother, Father, and Son, others as Mother, Father, and Daughter. The Triad that most Managements opt for, however, is VIRGIN, Mother, and CRONE.

3. Many Gods. This entails the worship of whole tribes of Gods, good and bad, who sometimes quarrel bitterly among themselves. The Rule here is that people always believe in the whole lot of Gods, but devote themselves, often quite fanatically, to just one. On some Tours, these Gods are spread out over several countries, to which they act as patron deities, but most Tours have the pantheon gathered into one CITY for convenience. This City will boast a TEMPLE for each God, each with its band of fervent and fanatical worshippers. Tourists should not miss

the religious processions here, which abound in quaint customs: leaping, dancing, cutting oneself, throwing oneself under the cart with the God in it, chanting, walking backwards, and many more things. Just occasionally, a particularly savage God worshipped in this City turns out to be in fact a DEMON imprisoned under a Temple. Where this is the case, the Management will always arrange for Tourists to descend and view the Demon in its pit.

There are two further absolute Rules for Religion:

i. All Gods fade away when their worshippers stop believing in them.
ii. However benign and Holy a belief is, or however zealously fanatics torture you, you as a Tourist will never, ever become a convert to any Religion you meet on a Tour.

See also IDOL and IMAGE.

**RELIGIOUS FEUDALISTS** have the same arrangements with HIGH PRIESTS as ARISTOCRATIC FEUDALISTS have with the bad KINGS, only in this case the ruler is the HIGH PRIEST. The inhabitants will go in terror of being accused of heresy, losing sons to the priesthood and daughters to the lusts of the clergy. This usually lasts until the Tour comes along and shakes them up. But expect one or two people you like to get crucified or burnt alive at the stake before you can reform this COUNTRY.

**RINGS** are as dangerously magical as SWORDS. Tourists should avoid putting on any Ring. If you have to acquire one as part of your QUEST, the safest way to wear it is on a thong round your neck. The Rules for Rings are as follows:

1. Rings with large carved stones, usually green, although sometimes a big ruby will do. These are fairly harmless,

since the carving is the crest or totem of the owner's family. The main thing these do is to prove your right to a Kingdom or lordship. Often the wrong person recognises it. Then you are in Trouble.

2. Rings with CRYSTAL stones. These need only be raised in anger for the Crystal to shoot FIRE and POWER and blast the people in front of you. This is awkward if you happen to lose your temper with a friend. And a further trouble is that these Rings need recharging frequently and will often not work when you really need them to.

3. Rings with a dead black stone. These are usually *accursed* OMT in some way and will either drain your spirit or allow the DARK LORD to take over your mind. Avoid these, no matter what other useful things they do.

4. Rings with any other kind of stone. Most of these will have belonged to WIZARDS or ELVES and the very least they will do is allow you MINDSPEECH with someone unexpected. Those with blue-green stones will either transport you abruptly elsewhere or put you in touch with some GODDESS. Some need only be turned around on the finger for unexpected things to happen. If you must wear one of these, avoid fidgeting with it. You may suddenly turn into a DRAGON.

5. Plain Rings with RUNES on the inside. Avoid these like the PLAGUE. The Rule is that, the plainer a Ring is, the more powerfully MAGIC and *accursed* OMT it will be.

**RITES** take place in TEMPLES, on hilltops at full MOON, and in other places designated by tradition at the start of the Tour; they especially take place in front of IDOLS (gorily) and IMAGES (with a certain twee impressiveness). If GOOD, Rites involve singing, a procession and a ceremony both charming and solemn. If EVIL (and these are in the majority), they take place in darkness and involve chanting, SACRIFICE, and bloodshed. All are religious services to honour or placate a deity. The Rules allow the Tour to interrupt Evil Rites but never Good ones.

**RIVERS** are frequent and wide. As so many Tours take place in winter, they are also usually *swollen* OMT and *turbid* OMT. The near absence of BRIDGES makes them rather a nuisance to the Tourist. You will have to cross them, which may mean going miles to find either somewhere shallow enough to ford or, conversely, a FERRYMAN. It will be night when you find one of the latter, and he will be very surly about getting you across; he may then betray you to the forces of the Dark who are following you. On the bright side, Rivers are long, deep, and wide, and there are often BOATS plying up and down them. If your Tour happens to lie down- or upriver, then you can save much time and effort by hitching a lift on a River-boat. River folk may likewise betray you, but they are, unlike Ferrymen, cheerful and colourful, and some are even GOOD (see COLOUR CODING and TRAVELLING FOLK).

**ROADS** in Fantasyland are not good. Tourists have frequent cause to complain. There are several types of Road, each with its characteristic inconvenience:

1. Ancient magical ways, normally engineered from some black rocklike substance impervious to wear. These are so old that only short stretches remain. The rest has been torn up or buried in some ancient CATACLYSM. This can be exasperating. You are just beginning to make some decent mileage on this tarmaclike surface when it stops, and you are back to a snail's pace again.

2. ANCIENT ENGINEERING PROJECTS. These are wider than an eight-lane highway, dead straight, and made of cobbles

**R**

## MORE ON RIVERS

RIVERS in Fantasyland are often very peculiar. Some even flow uphill. Setting aside normal features such as the fact that neither WITCHES nor the forces of the Dark are able to cross RIVERS, we are left with the unaccountable way that each bank of a given RIVER is liable to be different, and the even more unaccountable way the local inhabitants (**OMT** *dwellers*) ignore this oddity. The reason seems to be that the left bank of a River (facing downstream) is often Highly Magical and full of Hidden Dangers, so that the dwellers are unable to see that side of the River at all. Heaven knows what they think they see instead, or the reason for the difference between the two banks. Although it is always the left bank that is different, we can assume that the reason is not political.

that *preternaturally* **OMT** show no sign of ageing. Though hardly ever used today—they are characterised by windswept emptiness—they were clearly built to allow a traffic of horse-drawn carts, four lanes in each direction, travelling at seventy miles per hour.

3. Old trade routes. These are long-disused and normally serve to do little more than point you in the right direction. If you try to follow them you are quite likely to get lost when the route peters out into pathless moorland or even MARSHES. If the route is obvious, you will find no shelter along it, and no WATER.

4. Vestigial Roads of the VESTIGIAL EMPIRE. These cover quite a lot of the country and were once good roads made of stone blocks, but, in places from which the Empire has withdrawn, no maintenance has been done for centuries

and most of the stones are missing or broken. It rains a lot along these roads and the going gets rough. If you are lucky you may find tumbledown remnants of old guard-posts along the way, and these will provide some shelter; but don't count on it. As these roads approach what now remains of the Empire they are discovered to be in better repair and, closer to the Imperial capital, the guardposts are intact and well manned. Though this means you are safe from BANDITS you are not safe from the GUARDS, who at the sound of hooves will come out with demands for toll and bribes, and generally attempt to hassle you.

5. Unpaved roads. These are the norm. They are always muddy and full of deep ruts from the passage of MER-CHANTS and previous Tours. They lead through danger-ous WOODS and abound in *rocky defiles* **OMT** ideal for AMBUSH. Nobody ever maintains these, despite frequent representations to the Management, and you have to use them because they are the only way to get about. Some Tourists lose patience and ride across country, but this is not recommended because it is the surest way to get at-tacked by APELIKE CANNIBALS.

**ROBES** are the only garments, apart from SHIRTS, ever to have sleeves. They have three uses:

1. As the official uniform of PRIESTS, Priestesses, MONKS, Nuns (see NUNNERY), and WIZARDS. The OMT prescribed for the Robes of Priests and Nuns is that they *fall in severe folds*; of Priestesses that they *float*; and of Wizards that they *swirl*. You can thus see who you are dealing with.

2. For KINGS. The OMT here is *falling in stately folds*.

3. As the garb of DESERT NOMADS. The OMT has the Robes *covering them from head to foot*. (See DESERT NOMADS for a discussion of a possible TABOO here.)

**ROOTS** appear to be edible only in the MARSHES, where the Marshfolk find them by some means unknown to everyone else and dig them up to offer Tourists. These Roots are long, gluey, pallid, gritty, and mud-covered. But they make a change from STEW and WAYBREAD.

**RUINS** of former days, like ANCIENT ENGINEERING PROJECTS, litter Fantasyland. Only the large kind are important to the Tour, and even most of these will be just setting the mood. You are not expected to be happy on this Tour. The Ruins make you think of the sad losses of former days. But cheer up. Just occasionally you will find TREASURE in a Ruin.

**RUNES** are an intensely magical form of writing. Anything written in Runes is going to be a SPELL.

1. In GRIMOIRES. If the Spell is in Runes it will do its best to leap up and hit the Tourist reader, or at the very least sort of scintillate. In such cases, Runes have a way of translating themselves, so you may learn the Spell without wanting to.

2. In INSCRIPTIONS on rock. These are useful. Runes incised into cliffs reveal the presence of a hidden doorway or, particularly if inscribed on STONE CIRCLES, show that supernatural protection is available. Just occasionally, though, they show that entry is forbidden. Ask your Tour MENTOR.

3. In Fortune Telling. Here the Runes are written on little wooden buttons and thrown. The patterns they fall into are as important as the individual meaning of each letter. The Management, however, reserves the right to alter the significance of both without notice. See PROPHECY.

4. In Spellcasting. MAGIC USERS draw Runes all over PENTAGRAMS and around MAGIC circles as a prelude to im-

R

portant Magics. Some ADEPTS draw them inside other shapes, even more potently. Most WIZARDS incorporate Runes into the GESTURES they use, in which case they will briefly appear *glowing in the air*(OMT). We see from this that Runes do not need to make words in order to be powerful. The OMT here is *Runes of Power*.

5. Hidden. These Runes have to be made visible either by a Magic User passing her/his hands across them, by the application of heat, or by the light falling on them in a certain way. Runes of this kind tell anyone their message after that. But Wizards can leave hidden Runes written on walls that are only visible *glowing in the air*(OMT) to other Wizards. Hidden Runes are always extremely important.

6. Written on RINGS and SWORDS. These Runes always make words and nearly always mean trouble. Avoid any artifact with Runes on it, even if the Runes prove only to spell the maker's name.

R

# S

*Settle for what you can get, but first ask for the World.*

Ka'a Orto'o,
**Gnomic Utterances,** *C iv*

**SACRIFICE** is made both in TEMPLES and as an aid to the BLACK ARTS. In its minor form it involves cutting the throat of an ANIMAL, usually a goat. The major and preferred form is of course the ritual killing of a human, preferably young, female, and beautiful. This is normally done in a dim reddish light—to the accompaniment of chanting—and on an ALTAR. The victim is roped down, ritually raped, and then disembowelled. Someone has to stand at one end of the Altar to catch the blood, which has many uses in RELIGION and MAGIC. This kind of Sacrifice is frequently interrupted by a rescue party. Uninterrupted Sacrifices are much more sinister and complicated. Here the Tour will come upon the scene only after the Sacrifice has been performed, to find the *ritually mutilated* OMT corpse hanging piteously in its ropes on the Altar. A pause is usually allowed here, while you bury the corpse.

**SADDLE ROLL** is what the Rules state you have to have

for luggage; saddlebags are the only alternative. This is fine until your last HORSE is killed.

See also BACKPACKS.

**SAGA.** This is another word for your Tour, particularly if it goes on for several brochures.

**SAGE.** A wise and Holy man who died a long time ago. No one modern qualifies.

**SAVING THE WORLD** is something many Tours require you to do. You have to defeat the DARK LORD or WIZARDS who are trying to enslave everyone. It is about the same as a QUEST, except there is always a WAR, a personal CONFRONTATION, and a CATACLYSM before you succeed. Thousands of troops and DEMONS must be annihilated. The CITADEL or base of EVIL must be destroyed (*razed* **OMT**). This usually triggers a semi-natural disaster. Sometimes large parts of the world you are saving go up in smoke.

**SCALY FOLK**—apart from Dragons—are numerous and of all sizes from knee-high to a towering ten feet or more. They divide into lizard kinds, who live on land in warm climates, and fishy-snaky kinds, who live in the sea. These latter always have a telltale web between their fingers. All walk upright like humans. All are intelligent and many can do MINDSPEECH. Quite a few are very wise as well. If, however, the Management calls them *subtle* **OMT** this means they are not friendly to Tourists. Scaly Folk can appear as servitors or as advisors with useful KNOWLEDGE, but for some reason they never become COMPANIONS on the Tour. This may be because they are cold-blooded.

**SCENERY.** See LANDSCAPE and the cover of any brochure. The Tour will pass through a lot of Scenery, but no one will have much time to admire it.

**SCEPTRES** are, in Fantasyland, much more than mere regalia. They are a Royal version of a WIZARD's STAFF, made vastly more potent by being impregnated with Royal powers over generations of monarchs. Luckily they respond only to one of Royal blood. But, since they are so potent, someone has usually taken the Sceptre away and hidden it. The Tour will QUEST to recover it. Sometimes it is far away in a cave or underground fastness, only happened upon by accident; sometimes it is concealed by cunning MAGIC in the PALACE itself. In this case, the Tour must infiltrate the Palace and deceive the REGENT or usurper into letting them search the place. This search is made more difficult by the fact that Sceptres can disguise the way they look and slot into the furniture as if they were part of it. Normally only when the hand of the true heir (likely a MISSING HEIR) is laid upon it will a Sceptre reveal itself. It will be a sort of golden truncheon with a large STONE or CRYSTAL at the top. Some have little wings near the bottom.

**S**

**SCHOOL OF WEAPONRY** is to be found in most TOWNS belonging to ARISTOCRATIC FEUDALISTS and outside any MERCENARY winter quarters. The school will be in a house that is impressively neat, well maintained (often with vines trained up the walls), and very civilized. There will be a bare gymnasium with a good floor and an outside PRACTICE RING with a superb surface: everything in apple-pie order, in fact. A huge variety of training WEAPONS will hang from walls in neat rows. But the instruction and training given, though wholly excellent, will be very expensive. The Rule here is that the

Tourist will not be able to afford any lessons and so will be forced to act as a sparring partner for pupils at the school. Be prepared to receive painful blows and many bruises. But it will pay off. In a remarkably short time you will be able to defeat the School's star pupil and give a good account of yourself to the WEAPONMASTER himself. You will be glad of this when you are enslaved and forced to fight as a GLADIATOR.

**SCROLLS** are important sources of information about either HISTORY or MAGIC, and are only to be found jealously guarded in a MONASTERY or TEMPLE. You will usually have to steal your copy. Against this inconvenience is the highly useful fact that the Information in the Scroll will be wholly correct. There is, for some reason, no such thing as a lying, mistaken, or inaccurate Scroll.

**SCURVY.** Despite a diet consisting entirely of STEW and WAYBREAD, supplemented by only the occasional FISH, you will not suffer from this or any other deficiency disease. It is possible that, while on the Tour, you absorb vitamin C through the pores of your skin.

**SEA MONSTERS** are always vast, of whatever kind. You will see the odd Kraken, a Leviathan or so, and a sea serpent in huge loops, each one capable of wrapping itself around a SHIP. Most of them do no permanent harm: you will only be shipwrecked, and after clinging to a spar for a few days you will come to land.

**SEA PEOPLE** can be normal SCALY FOLK, but there are quite a few other kinds. The most common of these are the quasi-human:

1. Mermaids and mermen (*Merfolk* **OMT**). These seem to

have given up tempting mariners to their deaths and are generally friendly.

2. SHAPESHIFTING people. These often manifest as seals, but in some cases can be whales, dolphins, or fish. The Management refers to them impartially as *Selkies*; this means "seals," but must here be considered a technical term. Selkies are often fey and as hard to understand as MYSTICAL MASTERS, but if they appear in human form it is always because they have something important to tell you. See BAYS for where to contact them.

**SEASONS** in Fantasyland appear to be the normal Spring, Summer, Autumn (sometimes called Fall by the Management), and Winter, but few Tours get to see them all. The Management tends to start you out in late Autumn, by tradition, and you will then experience only Winter. Your perceptions are messed up anyway, because you will be travelling into hot climates and cold, as well as traversing many magical microclimates. You may as well give up wondering what the Season is and think of it all as WEATHER.

S

**SECRET.** A Secret of some sort is quite usual on a Tour. There are four main kinds:

1. Objects that must be kept Secret. These are stolen SCROLLS, RINGS, AMULETS, and most other QUEST OBJECTS. You will not want ENEMIES to know you have these. Some, like ORBS and SWORDS, insist on shining in public and have to be muffled in blankets. Oddly, most Objects try to reveal themselves in INNS.

2. Personal Secrets. Some COMPANIONS will not want their gender or their Royal birth known (see BIRTHRIGHT). Others will be of a nation or calling that could get them killed. For instance, WITCHES must generally be Secret in

## WHAT TO DO WHEN TAKING THE SECOND BROCHURE OF YOUR TOUR

This is the one where the Management has largely run out of ideas. It has lots of ideas for your third Tour, such as the Final Confrontation, the End of the World, and so forth, but for now it is simply marking time until then. If unchecked, it will cause you merely to rush about Fantasyland, doing nothing very much. You must

1. Bully your Tour MENTOR.
2. Bully her/him into taking you to lots of interesting places such as The Caves of Mourning, The Cataracts of Blindness, and The Many-Coloured Land.
3. Make sure you collect many more QUEST OBJECTS.
4. Bully your Tour Mentor into discovering a minor DARK LORD in a secondary CITADEL somewhere, so that you can usefully destroy her/him, preferably by invoking the Forces of Nature.

Even so, at the end of this Tour, you are liable to find yourself back more or less where you started, waiting for the Big One.

RELIGIOUS FEUDALIST Countries. Or Other PEOPLES will have to go to great lengths to conceal their hairiness from xenophobes (see XENOPHOBIA) in the FANATIC CALIPH-ATES. Or the entire Tour will for a while have to pretend allegiance to a bad KING for safety, and their real allegiance must be kept Secret.

3. Magical Secrets. These are either SPELLS or formulae necessary to the QUEST, which must usually be wrested from a WIZARD or a GRIMOIRE, or Magical Rules withheld by the Management for a later surprise. This is where you will find your Tour MENTOR especially maddening, because she/he will have known all along.

4. Vital Secrets. These are Secrets that cost lives. They can be the Secret way into a PALACE or CASTLE (see, for example, SECRET PASSAGES); the mustering of a Secret ARMY by the DARK LORD; the Secret substitution of the true PRINCE by a lookalike; the Secret conquest of a CITADEL/COUNTRY; a crucial and Very Secret weakness in the Dark Lord; or Secret KNOWLEDGE about the way the Gods made the world.

**SECRET PASSAGES.** No CASTLE, CITADEL, PALACE, or TEMPLE is complete without a lot of these, and very useful they are too. Although many Secret Passages are in the cellars or DUNGEONS, so that the release and escape of prisoners can be easily effected, there are usually just as many within the thick walls of the upper storeys. The upper Passages will be reached by pressing in a certain place on a wooden or stone wall carving, whereupon a narrow door will creak open to reveal a ladderlike stair. This will take you to the Passages in the walls of the COUNCIL Chamber and bedchambers, each provided with its concealed spyhole and listening space. If you go this way, you are bound to hear something important about your QUEST or Mission or discover that someone you thought friendly is plotting your downfall. You may also find your boyfriend making love to the QUEEN. Be careful not to rush away then in a state of shock: the Secret Passages are a maze and you will soon become lost. Usually the Management has thoughtfully provided you with a COMPANION on this jaunt who knows the Passages like the back of her/his hand, and you will be able to leave at once by the underground route through the SEWERS.

Tourists should note, however, that Secret Passages are useful to the forces of EVIL too. Be wary of what you say inside any BUILDING with thick walls. Someone is usually standing at the spyhole listening in. SECRETS are safe only when told inside a TENT.

See also UNDERGROUND PASSAGES.

**SEER.** A Talented old man or young woman able to see into the future (see PROPHECY and TALENT). They are either blind with *white eyes*  or tend to wear a symbolic blindfold. Having the GIFT OF SIGHT does not make Seers at all happy. Young female Seers are usually morbid and neurotic. Old men seem to have adjusted better, probably from having learnt there is nothing they can do about what they *See* .

**SELF-KNOWLEDGE** is, on rare occasions, a QUEST OBJECT. It is seldom found, and then only by PRINCES. Tourists are not expected to acquire it.

**SERIOUS SOLDIER** is a rather boring Tour COMPANION, although a very efficient one. He is even better at his job than the FEMALE MERCENARY and speaks even less. He is usually on the Tour to guard someone, and has no interest in it otherwise. Nevertheless you will miss him when he is killed.

**SEWERS.** Despite the presence of so much REFUSE and SQUALOR, most CASTLES and CITIES seem nowadays to have Sewers. Their use, apart from the obvious one, is to provide access to or escape from the interior. Be warned. Many Tours make use of Sewers in preference to SECRET PASSAGES. Opportunities for WASHING afterwards are not always provided. Do not worry, though: most often, within half a day, all trace of stench will have vanished from you and your CLOTHING, almost as if the Management had forgotten about it.

**SEX** is obligatory at some stage in the Tour. The Rules differ according to whether you are male or female. If male, your partner will be either an ever-youthful WITCH or some other beautiful and obliging female, possibly a female SLAVE. In any case you will not be obliged to feel any emotion and no offspring will result. If female, you are required to have strong feelings for your partner, who will usually be worthy of your regard. Again, there will be no offspring. Female Tourists should note that they will not menstruate during the Tour. Both sexes will be glad to know that sexually transmitted diseases are unknown.

See also BATH.

**SHAMAN** is another word for "charlatan" in Fantasyland. This pretended MAGIC USER will be dirty and strung about with little hairy bags. He will mumble a lot and produce useless information. An honest Shaman is unknown, although many seem to believe in their own powers. An exception to this is the Magic User you will find among the DESERT NO-MADS. She/he will sometimes be called a Shaman, but this is only because the true job description—MAGICIAN-SEER-PRIEST-HEALER-and-any-other-odd-magic—is a little long-winded. When you meet this person, you will see that she/he is in no way to be compared to the usual kind of Shaman.

**SHAPESHIFTING** is frequent among both WERES and MAGIC USERS. The usual form taken is that of a WOLF (see also WEREWOLVES), but lions, eagles, serpents, owls, and cats are common too. In all cases the Rule is that the Shape-shifter cannot stay too long in ANIMAL form without actually becoming that Animal and losing touch with her/his human thoughts. There are two schools of Shapeshifting:

1. Illusory. Here the shifter either pretends to have or has thrust upon her/him the appearance of an Animal. You

will drop to all fours but not lose your clothes. It is very important not to believe in this ILLUSION—otherwise you may go for days on hands and feet and get blisters and a cricked neck. A better form of this is to take the appearance of a piece of furniture. You will be far less ready to believe you are a table or a cupboard.

2. Actual. Here you really are the Animal or thing. In this case it is better not to become furniture. You will end up being an armchair for the rest of your life. There are two methods here:

   A) Change on land from human to Animal. This is normally swift and painless, though some Weres seem to suffer rather as their faces turn inside out. However, the most you will feel is discomfort and disorientation, shortly replaced by a wonderful sense of SMELL or the realization you can fly. The problem here is your clothes. They will not Shift with you and must be discarded. When you change back you will be naked.

   B) Change at sea. This often involves donning or discarding the skin of a seal, dolphin, or walrus. This skin must be stashed carefully on the beach. If someone gets hold of it you will not be able to turn back.

There is an absolute Rule that any wounds sustained in another form go back with you into human form.

**SHIELDS** are of four kinds:

1. Big oblong ones used by soldiers of the VESTIGIAL EMPIRE to protect them in fighting.
2. Round ones hung along the sides of SHIPS run by BARBARY VIKINGS.
3. Large, hastily assembled protection for ARMIES attacking WALLED CITIES.

4. Psychic.
5. No one else uses a Shield at all. This is odd, given the amount of fighting that goes on.

 **SHIPS.** The Rule is that PIRATE Ships are faster than any-thing—except that BARBARY VIKINGS, when on the side of GOOD, can overtake even PIRATES.

See also BOATS and GALLEYS.

 **SHIRTS** are always of thin material with long, floppy sleeves. They are normally worn without UNDERWEAR, and do not seem very warm. If you are prone to feel the cold, you are advised not to visit the SNOWBOUND NORTH (see FROSTBITE, HYPOTHERMIA, and WEATHER).

 **SHOPS** have not been invented yet, even in the VESTIGIAL EMPIRE. Visit the MARKET instead.

 **SIEGE** is when the ENEMY surrounds a CITY or TOWN (es-pecially a WALLED CITY) and tries to break down the walls. The Rule is that no besieger is ever content just to CAMP round the City and starve the defenders out. Tour sched-ules do not allow time for this. Instead, the Enemy throws soldiers under SHIELDS, battering rams, and Siege engines at the walls continuously, while the defenders shoot arrows from the walls and repel from the battlements soldiers scal-ing Siege towers and ladders. A lot of people on both sides get wounded. The defenders eventually run short of arrows but not of FOOD and Pluck. No one is forced to eat rats or HORSES. But the Enemy eventually breaches the walls and rampages around the City, killing, raping, and looting. No Siege is ever called off. Tourists, however, always escape through SECRET PASSAGES.

**SIGHT** is the TALENT of being able to *See* OMT into either the future or the past, or in a more general divinatory way into the workings of MAGIC or human politics and emotions. It is useful, but it can be a great burden to the possessor.

See also SEER.

**SILK** is worn quite frequently by the richer classes. It follows that somewhere in the land there must be a considerable and sophisticated silk industry (for instance, the OMT to describe the silk dresses of most female SLAVES is *diaphanous*, which argues considerable refinement among the producers), but the Tour will never take you anywhere near places where silkworms are cultivated. The Management wishes to keep some secrets.

See also INSECTS.

**SING** is used in a technical sense. This is because MUSIC is so powerful in Fantasyland that no one can really just Sing a SONG without risking a Magical result.

The most frequent use of Singing is to speed a dead person's soul on its way. On some Tours no one is properly dead without it (see UNDEAD). Otherwise Singing is an invocation, a SPELL, or a way of summoning nature MAGICS for some purpose. Tourists should be careful to avoid humming a casual tune. You may find you have summoned an ELEMENTAL, a STORM, or a selection of GODDESSES AND GODS.

**SKIRTS** are of five kinds, most to the ankle or below:

1. Coarse HOMESPUN, as worn by peasant women to show that they will be taking no real part in the action.
2. SILK, worn by women of high birth to show that they are malicious and/or demanding.

3. SILK, worn by women of very high birth to show that they are helpless pawns.

4. Gauzy, split to the hip, showing the wearer to be a SLAVE and/or dancing girl, or else a WITCH in seduction mode.

5. Little leather skirts worn by imperial GUARDS of the VESTIGIAL EMPIRE, showing how hardy they are.

**SLAVES, FEMALE,** are of three kinds, probably:

1. Tourists who have been captured by PIRATES or BANDITS. The Rules here state that such females must be lightly chained, loaded as soon as may be into a fairly small SHIP, and ferried to the OTHER CONTINENT. From this description you will see that this is the way female Tourists must proceed in order to take in that part of the Tour (see GALLEY SLAVE for the male route). Arrived at the Other Continent, you will be put up for auction in the Slave MARKET. You may well be annoyed to find how little your new owner pays for you, but this is the Management's way of protecting you from rape, beatings, and other hardships. Your purchaser will bring you to her/his villa (a building of one storey, mostly built of wood and covering a lot of ground) and there you will be put to work. You may even learn some useful skill, such as pastry-making or weaving. Alternatively, you might use the time to learn the alphabet of this continent (see HIEROGLYPHS) or study MAGIC. Make full use of this opportunity. Shortly, the villa will be raided by a CLAN that is feuding with your owner, and burnt down. You may use the resulting chaos to escape and continue your Tour.

2. Beautiful young women. You will find these in droves in the FANATIC CALIPHATES and sometimes in the PALACES of bad KINGS. Their duties are light and plea-

sant and are: looking beautiful, bathing and massaging visitors, singing and dancing, and, for male Tourists, providing company in bed. None of them seem unhappy in their work and they show no desire to escape. It is not usually possible to discover their life stories, but sometimes one will tell you that her father was a MERCHANT and that she was kidnapped by BANDITS somewhere many hundreds of miles away and was forced to watch her father being killed before she was carried off. Few seem to have been born to slavery.

Often male Tourists will sympathize with the plight of such Slaves, nobly reject their offer of free, no-holds-barred SEX, insist on assisting them to escape from the exploitative tyranny under which they have been existing, and then, having obviously done them a Good Turn, have free, no-holds-barred Sex before stranding them in the middle of nowhere to make their way thousands of miles back to their own COUNTRY.

3. Drudges. These exist, but are seldom seen. There must be someone who does the dusting, polishing, and laundry required in a large PALACE, as there must also be some occupation needed for beautiful young Slaves who are no longer beautiful or young, but you will not get to meet any. In fact, the only time you will become aware of drudges will be when you need to escape the Palace. You will still not meet one, but you will find a closet where drudges' clothes are hanging. When you put these on, you will gain the same INVISIBILITY as the drudge, and can simply walk away. Why all the drudges do not do exactly this is a SECRET of the Management.

**SLAVES, MALE,** are used by bad KINGS, FANATIC CALIPH-ATES, and some WIZARDS in large numbers as GUARDS, attendants, fan-bearers, waiters and entertainment, and for SEX. Bad Kings and Fanatic Caliphates always have their male Slaves in matching sets, as in *a litter borne by four gigantic ebony slaves* OMT, *fanned by two beautiful young boys* OMT, *a troupe of slender young acrobats* OMT, *the door guarded by two seemingly identical Barbarian slaves* OMT, etc. A Wizard tends to have his Slaves more mismatched but rather more attentive, unless he intends to rule the world, in which case he will try to be like a bad King.

See also EUNUCHS.

**SLENDER YOUTH.** A Tour COMPANION who may be either a lost PRINCE or a girl/PRINCESS in disguise. In the latter case it is tactful to pretend you think she is a boy. She/he will be ignorant, hasty, and shy, and will need hauling out of trouble quite a lot. But she/he will grow up in the course of the Tour. In fact she/he will be the only Companion who will change in any way. Quite often, she/he will soon exhibit a very useful TALENT for MAGIC and end up by hauling everyone else out of trouble. But this will not be until midway through your second brochure.

S

**SMALL MAN** can be a very funny or very tiresome Tour COMPANION, depending on how this kind of thing grabs you. He gambles (see GAMING), he drinks too much, and he always runs away. Since the Rules allow him to make JOKES, he will excuse his behaviour in a variety of comical ways. Physically he is stunted and not at all handsome, although he usually dresses flamboyantly. He tends to wear hats with feathers in. You will discover he is very vain. But, if you can avoid smacking him, you will come to tolerate if not love him. He will contrive, in some cowardly way, to play a major part in SAVING THE WORLD.

**SMELLS** are everywhere and strong, and, except for those of ENCHANTRESSES and INCENSE, unpleasant. Even DANGER has a Smell—the *REEK OF WRONGNESS* OMT. There is something in the chemistry of the land that makes Smells. It is probably a fallout effect of MAGIC, but see also SOCKS and TROUSERS.

**SNOWBOUND NORTH** is the COUNTRY beyond the most northerly MOUNTAINS where the NORTHERN BARBARIANS live. It is quite often the place where the DARK LORD chooses either to sequester himself or to plant a MUTANT NASTY of huge proportions whose magical exudations poison the whole continent. Therefore it is a very important place and the Tour will unfailingly call there. Do not expect a pleasant time. You will have to gatecrash a PALACE of ice and/or torch the Nasty. And contend with deep snow, blizzards, and Barbarians.

See also CHILBLAINS and HYPOTHERMIA.

**SOCKS** are never worn in Fantasyland. People thrust their feet, usually unwashed, straight into BOOTS.

**SONGS** in Fantasyland perform the same function as LEGENDS. If you are made to attend to the words of a Song, this is because they contain KNOWLEDGE you need. The tune is not important.

See also MUSIC and SING.

**SORCERY** is sometimes a general word for MAGIC, usually connected with *wiles* OMT, but also sometimes a technical term, referring to that part of Magic entailing the storage and use of POWER. In the latter case, the Sorcerer becomes a sort of battery.

**SOUL.** Your Soul is at risk from the moment you enter Fantasyland. If you are not shortly possessed by a DEMON or simply by another person (in both cases you will keep hearing a second voice in your head, often quarrelling violently with you), you are liable to have your Soul snatched abruptly to the Astral Plane for various strange experiences, or find your Soul transformed in a variety of unpleasing ways. Failing this, you will be subject to Psychic Vampirism, where someone will drain you of the will to live. To avoid all this, you must get your TOUR MENTOR to put strong protections around your Soul at the outset.

**SPEECH.** On some Tours it is necessary to adopt a high-falutin form of Speech. Instead of saying, "I shall go out and take a look" you have to say, "I shall now walk forth and examine things without." This is tiresome to have to keep up. Even more tiresome are those PanCeltic TOURS where you have to keep remembering to say "Och aye" and "Top of the marnin' te ye." But these are the Rules.

See also LANGUAGES.

**SPELLS** can do almost anything. They usually involve chanting, GESTURES, and ritual, but these range from a simple, silly rhyme to hours of invocation accompanied by the drawing of symbols, according to the complexity required. Some Spells require HERBS and outlandish ingredients like fish-feathers. Many can be readied beforehand and cast with a final word, and quite a few of these can be seen floating through the air before they roost on the victim and take effect. This sort of half-life in Spells can be dangerous, particularly if the Spell is written down. It can enter the mind of its own accord.

See also ENCHANTMENT, MAGIC, and GRIMOIRES.

**SPIDERS** are rare. This is fortunate because they are always of enormous size and venom. They lair in certain WOODS and in CAVES, where shorter and slighter Tourists may be seriously inconvenienced by their gigantic webs made of sticky, rope-thick strands. Often only a special SWORD will cut these webs, and it usually takes two or more Tourists to defeat the Spider. The reason for the monstrous size of Spiders in Fantasyland is that their former prey, INSECTS, no longer exists (see also ECOLOGY), so that Spiders have been forced to evolve into something big enough to entrap DWARFS, GNOMES, and small succulent humans.

**SPIES** are as much part of life in Fantasyland as they are in our own world. The ARISTOCRATIC FEUDALISTS, FANATIC CALIPHATES, MERCHANT FEUDALISTS, and VESTIGIAL EMPIRE have Spies everywhere. Many HIGH PRIESTS and some PIRATES also maintain them. BANDITS plant one in every CARAVAN. And the DARK LORD and his MINIONS have Spies in all KINGS' courts. (See also BIRDS and UNPLEASANT STRANGER.) The majority of Spies will of course report by MAGIC, sometimes in MINDSPEECH, but usually by some Farspeaking device such as a RING, a CRYSTAL, or an ORB. Tourists must be prepared to be watched every inch of their way.

See also ENEMY SPIES.

**SPOON.** About the only EATING IMPLEMENT you are allowed apart from your own knife or DAGGER.

**SPORT.** The only real Sport is FIGHTS. Those who can, train fiercely and take on everyone. Those who can't watch GLADIATORS and lay BETS.

See also GAMES and GAMING.

**SQUALOR** is the OMT for "local colour." Mostly it occurs in TOWNS and SMELLS rather strong (*noisome* , *unspeakable* ), but it is in fact wholly innocuous and just there for show.

**STAFFS.** The magical implement of nearly all WIZARDS. Staffs are about five or six feet long and often twisted or *carven* with some kind of head or face at the top end. Bad Wizards tend to have Staffs that are black and made of no easily recognizable substance. The face at the top will be nasty and may bite or give electric shocks. GOOD Wizards have Staffs made from real, honest wood. Both kinds can ignite with blue MAGELIGHT when necessary. Depending on the Rules for MAGIC on this particular Tour, a Staff can contain all a Wizard's SPELLS, leaving him helpless without it; or be simply a convenient conduit for Magic; or have a life of its own.

**STALLIONS** are always ridden by KINGS and other important people. You get the impression that no one of any standing would be seen dead on a mare or a gelding. Luckily, the Stallions are quite docile about it. (See HORSES for the reason why these impressive beasts are so easy to control.)

**STANDING STONES.** See PORTALS, QUESTS, STONE CIRCLES, and STONES.

**STARS** are quite unlike those of Earth. For one thing, they seem to predict the future much more accurately than our own.

See also ASTROLOGY and ZODIAC.

**STARTING POINT** is where you commence your Tour. Having proceeded through your PORTAL to Fantasyland, you will find yourself either on the MAP in the neighbourhood of a small to medium TOWN, such as Gna'ash (immediately see SQUALOR), or in rather poor circumstances, usually those of a menial in a KITCHEN or an APPRENTICE to a BLACKSMITH (see SQUALOR again) in an unimportant corner of the continent. If you are in Gna'ash, you must at once set about acquiring COMPANIONS and equipment on your own. If you are in menial circumstances, you will be contacted by your Tour MENTOR (normally an elderly male MAGIC USER with much experience) who will tell you what to do, which is almost certainly to discover you are a MISSING HEIR and, after three brochures, to claim your rightful THRONE.

**STEPPES** are miles and miles of rolling grassland that suddenly happen some way south of the SNOWBOUND NORTH. They are a marvellous place for breeding HORSES, and the ANGLO-SAXON COSSACKS who live here do just that. But, since the Anglo-Saxon Cossacks do not find themselves able to live in TENTS, the Management has carefully strewn the grasslands with large outcrops of rock suitable for CITADELS and Dwellings. The result is *austerely picturesque* (OMT). The sole drawback here is the wind, which brings continual squalls of sleet and snow.

**S**

**STEW** (the OMTs are *thick* and *savoury*, which translate as "viscous" and "dark brown") is the staple FOOD in Fantasyland, so be warned. You may shortly be longing passionately for omelette, steak, or baked beans, but none of these will be forthcoming, indoors or out. Stew will be what you are served to eat every single time. Given the disturbed nature of life in this land, where in CAMP you are likely to be attacked without warning (but see BATH), and in an INN prone to be the centre of a TAVERN BRAWL, Stew seems to be an odd choice as staple food, since, on a rough calculation, it takes forty times as long to prepare as steak. But it is clear the inhabitants have not yet discovered fast food. The exact recipe for Stew is of course a Management secret, but it is thought to contain meat of some kind and perhaps even vegetables. Do not expect a salad on the side.

**STONE CIRCLES** are on some Tours quite a feature of the WASTE AREAS. Most are simple circles, but some can instantly turn into a maze when entered by the unwary. They can be GOOD or EVIL, and are given COLOUR CODING accordingly. A Good Stone Circle will be of either white or bluish STONES, which may have a RUNE carved on them somewhere to confirm this allegiance. Inside such a Circle a Tourist may travel to another place or be safe for the night from the forces of Dark, which will sniff round the edges but be unable to enter. Further to this, Good Stone Circles are a powerful aid to magically induced KNOWLEDGE and sometimes even to SELF-KNOWLEDGE. You can sometimes have quite an argument with one. After a night of defending your motives, you will come away wiser. Bad Stone Circles are of black Stones, *shine with an unwholesome sickly light* **OMT**, and are imbued with the *REEK OF WRONGNESS* **OMT**. Avoid entering these.

**STONES.** Some QUESTS prefer a spot marked by a Stone as the QUEST OBJECT. Such Stones can be on: an ISLAND, in which case the Tour will be met by ELVES, MYSTICAL MASTERS, or special guardians; a crag, in which case the Quest goes on after an interval for meditation and SELF-KNOWLEDGE; or in a remote spot or CAVE—this Stone will have an INSCRIPTION which ought to clarify things. Nearly all Stones are Quest Objects in the second brochure only. You will need to book another Tour after finding them.

**STORM CONTROL** can be exercised by most WIZARDS and many other MAGIC USERS, but even the most EVIL of these is remarkably conventional: rain, hail, snow, dust, ice, and wind are the only kind of STORMS raised. These are, of course, useful in their places, but not one Storm-raiser shows half the invention of, let us say, Moses. Rains of frogs, showers of blood, and Storm-borne locusts are practically unexploited.

**STORMS** are of three kinds. Not surprisingly, hardly a day passes without a Storm of some kind.

1.  Natural (see WEATHER). These are all the usual kinds, including dust storms. The Rule is that a Storm occurs when you least need it to. Storms at sea are likely to throw up both MONSTERS and whirlpools (*maelstroms* **OMT**).
2.  Magical (see STORM CONTROL). Here a WIZARD will have produced the MAGIC to make a natural-style Storm at the time and place it is needed. These are actually less inconvenient than the normal kind, unless the WIZARD is your Enemy, but also rather more severe.
3.  Storms of MAGIC. These are quite unpredictable to everyone. They occur when the lumps of loose Magic and/or the BACKLASHES to major SPELLS get out of control. They can be very violent and may last for days, during which time the very fabric of existence quakes, MAGIC USERS become sick or fall over, coloured lights manifest, sparkling MISTS swirl, and ANIMALS and plants are flung for many leagues. The Rule is that these Storms avoid major centres of population.

**STRANGE RACES** whose individuals are both aggressive and expendable turn up here and there in CAVES and TAVERN BRAWLS and aboard PIRATE Ships. They can be of any shape and size the Management chooses. Their main function is to get killed and to bleed blood of an unspecified *strange colour* OMT. Just occasionally, a Tourist succeeds in making friends with one of these PEOPLES, whereupon she/he will discover that Strange Races are almost human.

**SWORDS.** You are advised to choose your Sword with great care and, if possible, have it thoroughly checked by a jobbing MAGICIAN before undertaking ownership. Swords are *dangerous*. This does not simply mean that you can stab yourself in the foot with one without due care (though some Swords do that too, if crossed): it means that all Swords in Fantasyland are dangerously magical in some way. Here are the hazards you should look out for and avoid if possible:

1. Swords with RUNES. Runes are almost always a sign that your Sword is
   A) Designed only to kill DRAGONS.
   B) Designed for some other specific victim, such as GOBLINS or UNDEAD.
   Both A) and B) are likely to let you down if you are attacked by ordinary humans.
   c) Designed for some other purpose entirely, so that when drawn it will proceed to raise a STORM or— Gods protect you!—try to *heal* your assailant.

Be wary of Runes, even if they appear to say only "Made in Gna'ash."

2. Swords with Souls. These will contain
   A) The soul of someone formerly alive or, worse,
   B) A soul of their own.
   Swords of both A) and B) types are prone to argue with

you in MINDSPEECH whenever you are trying to use them to fight with. Since the Rules clearly state that all Swords are extremely old, your Sword's soul will be old too, and probably set in its ways. It will interrupt you and impair your concentration with antiquated advice. Or it could even be a pacifist; it will then declare that it has given up killing, and go all bendy.

   c) A highly aggressive soul. This kind of Sword tends to take over the user at unexpected moments, put her/him through impeccable but obsolete Martial Arts movements, and end up beheading people on rather slender grounds. This can be awkward. The relatives of the beheaded person may not be pleased, and there is a strong possibility the wielder may dislocate a joint through being forced to adopt an unaccustomed fighting posture.

3. Swords with appetites. These feed on:

   A) Blood.

   B) Lifeforce.

   c) Souls.

The preferred provender of any given Sword depends upon the whim of its maker. Some Swords are partial to all three and may, if not regularly fed, turn and feed on their owners. Fortunately, these Swords can be distinguished (and then quickly avoided) by their dead black unreflective colouration, their extreme coldness to the touch, and their unloveable habit of welding themselves to the hand of their future owner. Needless to say, by the time that has happened, it is too late. You are stuck with a hungry Sword.

4. Swords that give signals. This class of Sword heralds the approach of enemies by:

   A) Running with blood.

S

B) Groaning or singing.

c) Shining with an unearthly light or bursting into flame. This causes at least two kinds of trouble. In the first place, if there are ten enemies to one of you, you will certainly want to hide rather than face them, but the activities of your Sword will rapidly betray your hiding place. In the second place, the enemies of your Sword may not be your enemies at all, and it can cause you much embarrassment by dripping, shouting, or shining in front of your friends. If you must own a sword of this class, it is better to opt for Swords that

D) Merely turn icy cold. You can always wear a glove.

5. Swords that are something else. These will *look* like Swords, but are in reality made of some other substance entirely:

A) Star metal. This is like steel, but brighter. It not only holds a wicked edge, but you can cut through *anything*. This has its uses but, before you learn what these are, you may have lost a finger and several toes. Besides, this Sword will be continually slicing through its scabbard and plunging point-down into the earth. And it will go in a long way.

B) Forged of pure spirit, though goodness knows *how*. This Sword will usually resemble a bar of light, and like a genuine bar of light it is probably most useful as a torch for frightening nocturnal creatures (see LIGHTING). Rumour has it that it operates like a laser, but most experienced Tourists agree that it does this only in the Final CONFRONTATION with the DARK LORD.

c) A DEMON. The Demon will be standing very straight with its arms by its sides and be further disguised by ILLUSION. But it will have its demonic powers intact and, unless you know its NAME, or have other means of controlling it, it will get you in the end.

D) Glass. This is quite common, unpractical as such a sword might seem. It may be best to snap it off to a razor-sharp splinter straight away and use it as you would your DAGGER. Unfortunately, such Swords tend to belong to MYSTICAL MASTERS, who might object to this.

E) CRYSTAL. This must be a telepathic device in disguise.

6. Swords in stones. Avoid these at all costs. Usually such Swords are easy to spot because they will be up to half their length inside a rather large boulder, but Illusion may have been used to make the boulder look like a pebble on the very point. And they will be offered to you cheap because nobody else will want them. Resist the bargain. The sole use of such Swords is to acclaim you KING of some godforsaken Kingdom or other.

7. Swords that are incomplete.

A) With a notch or missing bit. This type will be pressed on you as an heirloom that has seen much service. It may even have belonged to your father. But there is a high probability that the missing fragment will turn up embedded in someone's head, arm, or leg and you could be accused of murder.

B) Broken into two or more pieces. This Sword will probably be given to you as useless. Or you will find it on a corpse in a forest clearing. Get rid of it at once. Before the Tour has lasted much longer, you will be required to reforge the bugger for a special purpose of a dangerous and frightening nature. First you will have to spend nearly a year learning metalwork and forging and then you will have to do the unpleasant thing the Sword has set you up for. It is not worth it.

S

8. Swords that contain your own magical powers. This is a stupid place to put your powers, but it can happen accidentally. This is why swords are so dangerous. If this has happened, seek magical aid at once and have the sword unzipped. If you have pumped the Sword full of your powers on purpose, there is no hope for you.

9. Swords that are gaudy. These can be very tempting, what with wavy patterns down the middle, bright metalwork, and big stones in the hilt. Do not be fooled. This pretty Sword could be:

   A) A dress Sword for Court that will not keep an edge. It will certainly break or crumple in serious use.

   B) CURSED, in any number of ingenious ways.

   c) Dangerous because of the big precious stones in the hilt. This keeps the Rule that all JEWELLERY in Fantasyland has some magical purpose. The big red stone could poison you. The large green stone could hypnotize you. And the great yellow stone is certainly a means for the DARK LORD or a MINION to whisper things to you that control you to their ends (*fell purposes* OMT). (See also MAGIC OBJECTS.)

10. Swords that seem quite innocuous. These can still turn out to be any of the above without warning.

We would advise against buying or using a Sword, except that in Fantasyland this would make you look as if you were walking in traffic with no clothes on.

*Tes'rac was an ordinary man who was no happier than the King. Tes'rac suggested to the King that they change places to prove it, but the King declined on the grounds that it was self-evident.*

*Ka'a Orto'o,*
**Gnomic Utterances,** *II v*

**TABOO** is something that is so sacred and so terrible that it cannot be changed, touched, or mentioned. This is why you will find no entry in *Toughpick* for the Rules.

**TALENT** is the technical term and OMT, although GIFT is sometimes preferred as a variation, for the inborn ability to do MAGIC. If it is a general ability for all Magic it is *High Talent* ⟨OMT⟩. If it is an ability to perform only one or two types of Magic, then it is used in the plural, as *His Talents were Firestarting and Mindspeech* ⟨OMT⟩. This OMT is never used of any other ability except MUSIC, which in Fantasyland counts as a magical Talent.

**TALENTED GIRL.** This young lady has almost constant employment as Tour COMPANION. The reason is that she not only has enormous potential as a MAGIC USER, which is something she has to learn about in the course of the Tour, but is good-looking with it, if you don't mind girls who are tall and skinny or else unusually short. She will have either red or fair hair and blue or green eyes (see COLOUR CODING) and a highly spirited and resourceful personality to go with these. This quite often causes her to argue with her Tour Companions. She is usually pretty opinionated, or will be as soon as she gets her confidence. Sometimes she will join the Tour quietly at the start, having set out to seek her fortune from the INN, but more often she will join from a VILLAGE or a PALACE. If she comes from a Village, she will have had some training from a local HERBWOMAN or BARD. When she comes from a Palace, she will be a PRINCESS or a Good QUEEN, and may or may not be trained. In all cases, there will be much still for her to learn. She is usually the Companion who must acquire the SECRET that will enable the Tour to succeed in SAVING THE WORLD.

**TALISMAN.** The same as AMULET, only Talismans do not hang round your neck.

**TAROT.** See PROPHECY.

**TAVERNS** are either in a cellar or open to the street, and mostly serve only bad cheap drink and very greasy STEW. MERCENARIES love Taverns, but the Management disapproves. The OMT is *low*. Most Tourists will enter a Tavern only in order to get disgustingly drunk for the first time, but be careful: about twenty percent of Taverns harbour an Assassin with a contract for you. Avoid Taverns unless you really want a terrible hangover or a bout of unarmed combat. Stick to INNS.

**TAVERN BRAWL.** This will break out without warning in any crowded TAVERN or INN early on in the Tour. The Rule is that everyone in the taproom almost instantly joins in, and the ferocity of the fighting is normally extreme. SWORDS, chair legs, and tankards may be used impartially. There will be a lot of shouting and crashing. The amount of actual injury is, however, usually minimal, unless members of STRANGE RACES happen to be present, in which case there will be large quantities of blood (*some of it an odd colour* OMT) and possibly a death or so, along with extensive breakages. Do not be alarmed. Be guided by the INNKEEPER, who will take it in his stride. If you feel like joining in, you may; but, if not, the Management will have arranged for you to find yourself either quickly underneath a table or else drawn gently by the elbow to a place of safety. The Rules also state that the next morning there will be little or no sign of the mayhem of the previous night.

**TEENAGE BOY** is a very young Tour COMPANION. He will  grow larger. Even to start with he is quite big, thin, and gan-  gling. This is because he is a MISSING HEIR or a thief (see THIEVES' GUILD) who has not had a decent start in life. He is very good-hearted and moderately clever, and a bit of a lunk with it. He will tend to throw up after FIGHTS; and this will not change, however big he grows. He will go on to inherit riches and/or a Kingdom and still be the same.

**TELEKINESIS** is the magical ability to move objects about  without touching them. It is done a lot, but it is not given this name. In fact, there is no OMT for Telekinesis.

**TELEPATHY.** See MINDSPEECH.

**TELEPORTING** is when a MAGIC USER moves himself (and  sometimes other people) from one place to another without touching the space in between. It is a very useful art which we have yet to learn in this world.

**TEMPLES** are richly architectured marvels. All Tourists should attempt to take in the grandeurs of at least one Temple, even though the Management will arrange for you to be very busy while you are there. Temples cover a great deal of ground and also occupy the skyline with ranks of sumptuous domes, painted, gilded, and carved with images, with minarets and twisty towers and sometimes steeples as well. They have gargoyles on every wall and coloured roofs with fretworked edges. Temples go deep underground too, in a labyrinth of DUNGEONS, TREASURE rooms, and SECRET PASSAGES. Each is enormously wealthy, some of them by highly questionable means.

The layout of a Temple is traditional. There will be an elaborate facade, sometimes frighteningly carved, with a gate in it guarded by fanatics. Inside the gate will be at least two forecourts, one thronged with people delivering offerings and/or protection money, the other thronged with Temple Prostitutes. PRIESTS will patrol here, looking for trouble, thieves, and pretty women to abduct as SLAVES. There may then be an inner court, smoking with small SACRIFICES.

Beyond that will be the public Temple, very large, with *ornate pillars* OMT and elaborately tiled floor. It will be dimly lit. Chanting will be going on. There will be an IDOL or IMAGE of the God here, but this may well not be the Image you are looking for—if you need to steal anything from Temple, be sure that this is not the Image you need. You will have to penetrate beyond, where the building becomes steadily more confusing and secret. First will come the quarters for NOVICES and GUARDS (*austere* OMT, *ascetic* OMT), then quite comfortable quarters for qualified Priests, and then the inner Temple. This is where the true, dark, fanatical worship goes on and the serious Sacrifices get made. The Idol here may be lit by a red light. This is the one you must look for if you need to steal any of its sacred regalia or JEWELS. If, however, it is a SCROLL you have to steal, you must go on, to the inner parts where the library (*musty*(OMT)) is to be found. A long way further inside from here, you will find the place where the HIGH PRIEST has made himself very comfortable indeed. Here also you will find the rooms for his concubines and catamites. This is the part you will have to get to if you need to rescue a COMPANION from his clutches. Go carefully. There are often magical traps.

Surprisingly, some Temples are not EVIL. You can tell because the High Priest will not have made himself comfortable. However, GOOD Temples are rare. And take care again. Some Evil High Priests are not above having falsely ascetic quarters to make people think they are holy. In such cases, expect an inner ring of initiates who will resent your foray and try to kill you.

**TENTS** are soundproof structures of canvas or skin that are hauled along when ARMIES or MERCENARIES are on the march. Good KINGS and their generals have large Tents, quite modestly furnished with a lamp, a bed, and a table covered with maps. Bad Kings and Mercenary captains have carpets and real furniture (of *nearly barbaric splendour*(OMT)) and dangling golden chandeliers. Their Tents are often divided into several rooms, for the use of servants, concubines, and prisoners; most of these are also fully furnished. It is hard to see how this lot gets carried from CAMP to camp, but somehow it does.

See also NOMAD TENTS.

**TERRAIN** varies enormously in Fantasyland, and with great abruptness. You can go from tilled land to magical WASTE AREA in a few steps, or from MARSHES to STEPPES in the same way. What is constant is that the going is terrible. Thus, in tilled land, the ROAD will be all muddy ruts, while on the Steppes there will be no Road and a strong keen wind; expect snow in any MOUNTAINS, stasis in the Marshes (even by BOAT), roots and tangled vegetation in a WOOD, BOGS, and steep hills near RIVERS, areas of gravel and boulders elsewhere. Perhaps worst, in the magical Waste Areas your way will be blocked by seeping slimes, ILLUSIONS, landslides, and magical MISTS. Only in the small area now occupied by the VESTIGIAL EMPIRE can you expect to travel with any freedom.

**THIEVES' GUILD.** The best organized body of people in the continent. Thieves' Guilds exist in all CITIES and can usually pass messages reliably between branches, although each City appears to have its own independent hierarchy. The Thieves' Guild exists to transfer wealth but not to distribute it. Its members are pickpockets, burglars, robbers, fences, and housebreakers, but never muggers. The Guild claims to be a body of artists. All its members profess horror at violence (but are quite proficient fighters all the same) and pride themselves on bringing off robberies in apparently impregnable TREASURE stores, on picking locks, and on climbing smooth walls. The Guild is organized into masters, journeymen, and APPRENTICES, with an anonymous Hidden Head, or Guildmaster, who rejoices in such NAMES as The Faceless Man or The Gentleman. You will be taken to see this person at some point when your Tour visits a City. You will be blindfolded and led along strange-smelling passages to an upstairs venue evidently concealed between two or more

T

houses. The man's face will be veiled by MAGIC or masked. But meanwhile you will have made the acquaintance of a very young Apprentice thief. In return for the Guild's helping the Tour, the Hidden Guildmaster will ask you to look after this Child because he shows promise, and you will take him with you when you leave on the rest of the Tour. He will become an excellent and useful Tour COMPANION, and even make JOKES. There is always an unspoken suggestion that this young thief is the son of the Hidden Guildmaster.

**THRONES** are the elaborate seats that KINGS, QUEENS, Evil WIZARDS, and Emperors sit in. They are usually of metal or stone and placed on a platform in the Throne Room. Metal Thrones are either of gold or of some metal symbolic of the ruler's nature. Thus a cruel and unforgiving King will have a Throne of IRON. A lovely young Queen will have one of silver. The metal will be worked with *consummate artistry* (OMT) into beasts, flowers, and abstract designs all over, and may be jewelled as well. Stone Thrones tend to be carved into ANIMAL shapes or austerely simple. Both kinds must be chilly and uncomfortable. It is therefore surprising how many rulers spend their leisure hours sitting on their Thrones, alone in the Throne Room, often wearing their Crowns as well. This is a convenient habit: when you are ready to overthrow an Evil King or Wizard, you at least know where to find him.

T

**TIME** taken on the Tour is often vague. Only if there is a public festival which happens all over the continent will you be able to tell how long you have taken getting anywhere. You may be slogging happily along and find yourself surprised that you have had *months of travel* (OMT). Or you may think you have been a year on the way and find it has been only days. The Management likes to keep you guessing.

**TOMBS.** There are few or no churchyards in Fantasyland, so Tombs tend to have to be in peculiar places. The Rule is that, wherever a Tomb is, it is always intensely sinister and normally visited at night. Tombs are:

1. On a hill outside a TOWN. Here there are always many Tombs. Tourists will visit by moonlight and become appalled by hootings, rustlings, and groaning. These are sound effects only, unless there is reason to expect a GHOST or VAMPIRES. You will be alerted to these by *a sense of dread*(OMT) or *a cold chill down the spine*(OMT). This will be followed by sight of *a white flitting shape*(OMT).

2. In one of the few churches. Here the Tomb is in a side chapel and will be approached when moonlight makes *strange coloured patterns on the floor*(OMT) from the stained-glass windows. Expect to be terrified here too.

3. On its own in open country. Here you will *decipher*(OMT) an INSCRIPTION that makes it clear that the occupant of this Tomb has KNOWLEDGE that you need. You must then engage a Necromancer (see NECROMANCY) who will raise something that looks uncomfortably like a decaying corpse to answer your questions. Even in broad daylight, this is a harrowing experience.

4. Somewhere in a catacomb. Here you will pass through UNDERGROUND PASSAGES lined with skulls and hipbones, to the accompaniment of rustlings and gurglings, until you reach an inner CHAMBER. Expect to get colder with every yard you go. In the Chamber there will be either a single Tomb with an INSCRIPTION you need to read, or a whole roomful, each with a statue of its contents. You will probably need to raise and talk to these occupants too.

5. In a RUIN or OLD RUINED CITY. Just occasionally the Ruin looks like a Pyramid. More often it is an antique

sort of TEMPLE. You will have to descend into this, either by stairs or by an excavated pathway, with the *sense of doom* OMT growing about you, and proceed by flaring torchlight to the centre of a tangle of passages. There will be *the dust of ages* OMT everywhere, but the age-old booby traps will still be in place. The Tomb will be in the middle of the central Chamber in front of an ALTAR and both will try to flame you or get you bitten by snakes. In some cases the buried person will manifest and try to stop you in person. She/he will definitely be of a STRANGE RACE and glowing unpleasantly. You have to disarm this antique MAGIC. The thing you are looking for will usually be behind or under the Altar. Do not waste time on the Tomb. It is there for misdirection only.

6. In a Barrow. Here, once you get inside, the corpse will be lying on a slab in the middle. Probably your arrival will trip the SPELL that arouses it. It will seem confused and attempt to equate your party with a set of marauders it knew centuries ago. It will try to kill you with its grave furniture. It may also attempt to take over your body for its own use. Barrows are the most unsettling Tombs of all.

**TORTURE** is obligatory at some stage on the Tour. Generally this takes the form of being tied to rings in the wall almost too high for you to reach, and then being flogged. But on occasions worse things happen. Tourists usually find the Management blanks their minds to the details afterwards.

See also CHAMBER, EXECUTIONS, and PRISON.

**TOUR** is everything here in *Toughpick*, plus any of a few variations the Management has devised. Most Tourists will need to spend up to six months recovering after they reach home.

**TOUR MENTOR.** See MENTOR and MYSTICAL MASTERS.

**TOWERS** (*brooding*⟨OMT⟩, *dark*⟨OMT⟩) stand alone in WASTE AREAS and almost always belong to WIZARDS. All are several storeys high, round, doorless, virtually windowless, and composed of smooth blocks of masonry that make them very hard to climb. The Rule is that there is also a strong no-entry SPELL, often backed up by a guardian DEMON. In addition, Towers are subject to COLOUR CODING: black for EVIL Wizards and blue, white, or red for GOOD or neutral ones. Black Towers tend to cast a blight of Evil on the surrounding TERRAIN: days before you reach them, you will have been able to tell they are near by the dead grass and TREES.

You will have to go to a Tower and then break into it at some point towards the end of your Tour. Usually by then you will have an AMULET or TALISMAN that will act as a key, but sometimes you may have to climb the Tower and force an entry on the roof. Inside, the Tower keeps the Rule about BUILDINGS and is much bigger, with many more floors, each of which suffuses your party in acid MISTS or ILLUSION or turns you into something nasty.

You have to stop this by breaking the central Spell. Hacking it apart with SWORDS usually suffices. This brings out the Demon. When you have dealt with the Demon, the Wizard himself will appear. If Evil, he will hurl far more subtle Spells at you. You will need to know a SECRET to stop him. If Good or neutral, he is quite likely to appear in a crystal box apparently asleep, and you will have to wake him. This can take days. Towers are quite arduous matters.

**TOWNS** are smaller than CITIES and do not always have walls; some may have palisades instead. A Town will be under the power of a lord, but will have a MAYOR for day-to-day

T

ruling. Otherwise the Rules for Cities apply. Expect at least one INCIDENT here.

> **TRANSFORMATION** has been defined as "inflicted metamorphosis" and is quite as uncomfortable as that sounds. Someone has, without asking you, turned you into a carthorse or a table with bendy legs. It usually takes a WIZARD to remove you from this discomfort.

**TRANSPORT.** Because of MAGIC and bad ROADS, Transport is very primitive. Here, though, are some general notes:

1. By land, if you do not ride a HORSE, you must go by cart or waggon. Both of these have wooden wheels and no springs. Carriages are known, but very rare, even in TOWNS. They have slightly more springing but are distressingly likely either to break down or to be waylaid by BANDITS. Tourists who ride in a carriage complain how chilly they are despite sheepskin coverings inside. Ladies and Evil WIZARDS prefer to travel instead by litter. This is a kind of curtained bed that can be slung between Horses, but most often is carried by a team of strong servitors or SLAVES. Litters are most frequently encountered in CITIES.

2. By WATER, whether sea or RIVER, you must go by small wooden BOAT, FERRY, RIVERBOAT, or SHIP. Whichever of these craft you find yourself on, be assured that one of the following will occur:

    A) It will sink, possibly because of attack by a SEA MONSTER; Sea Monsters are attracted by Tourists as mice are by cheese, although it is a lot easier to understand how the mice know the cheese is there than how the Sea Monsters know the Tourists are there. Perhaps

Tourists possess an identifying SMELL to which Sea Monsters are unusually sensitive. Even if there is no Sea Monster in the region, the Ship is likely destined for the bottom: why captains take Tourists on board at all is a mystery, in this context, unless they are confident of cleaning up on the Insurance.

B) You will be attacked by PIRATES, who will hack to death or hang all the crewmen who have no NAME and possibly the grizzled but kindly Captain as well, so that you can pause for a restorative tear or two before trying to reconcile yourself to the fact that you are now a SLAVE, bound to be either a GLADIATOR or a GALLEY Slave, if male, or towards An Even Worse Fate, if female (except that it will not be all bad because one of the people who rapes you/to whom you will be obliged to offer sexual favours will turn out to be somewhat fanciable and GOOD at heart, not to mention an exquisite lover, and will in due course help you escape).

C) You will be betrayed to the forces of the DARK LORD as soon as you have been either delivered to your destination or thrown off the vessel in disgust by the crew.

D) The Ship proves to be able to fly through the air rather than merely chug through the water. This will of course obviate your inborn tendency, as a Tourist, to seasickness: instead you will discover airsickness.

Travel by Water is not to be recommended, but you will certainly do it nevertheless—and more than once.

See also TELEPORTING and TRAVELLING FOLK.

**TRAVELLING FOLK** are quite common. They are of two kinds:

1. Land travellers, who go about in TRIBES in gaudily painted carts. These people are merry, colourfully dressed, dishonest, and knowledgeable. When you meet an encampment of them, they will cheat you, cure your wounds, feed you a variant of STEW, and then hustle you off to the cart of their oldest lady, who will tell you something about the future you need to know (see PROPHECY). After that you will spend time feasting and chatting with the rest. Listen carefully. Land Travellers know LEGENDS and SONGS which always turn out to be important.

2. RIVER travellers are equally gaudy, cheery, and dishonest. They have brightly painted BOATS which ply up and down Rivers and are navigated by *close-knit families* **OMT**. Tourists can either pay for a lift in the Boat, usually with the last of their MONEY, or stow away. In both cases the River travellers will be very grudging about it (although retaining their cheeriness) and force you to help in the chores. You will peel endless vegetables for STEW, haul ropes, and possibly do laundry as well. They will get even more grudging if the pursuing forces of the Dark catch up and try to damage the Boat. They will often tip you ashore and then tell the DARK LORD exactly where you went. Before that, they will have given you valuable Information either about the TERRAIN to come or in the form of a LEGEND. It is normally worth putting up with their clannishness (see CLANS) just for this.

**TREASURE** lies about in piles in Fantasyland, provided you know where to look. You should search for the following sources:

1. TOMBS, on which there is usually a CURSE.

2. DRAGONS' lairs, where the difficulties of removing the Treasure are obvious.

3. Deserted DWARVEN FASTNESSES, where the Treasure is likely to be in the form of ARMOUR of a make and fabric unknown to the present day (but which nevertheless fits you perfectly), or WEAPONS.

4. TEMPLE treasuries, where most of the Treasure will be MAGIC items, some of them unexpectedly dangerous, such as RINGS and CRYSTALS which put you in immediate touch with the DARK LORD.

5. The Treasure houses of KINGS. Except in the case of Puppet Kings and REGENTS, you are advised to let the King make his own selection of Treasure and give it to you freely. He knows the magical conditions that go with each item.

6. The cellars of ruined TOWERS/CITADELS, etc. Here only about half the Treasure will prove lethal.

7. Note that the Rule is that no Treasure in the form of MONEY can be retained for long, and that the only use it will be is to buy yourself an ARMY or pay your MERCENARIES.

**TREE HOMES** are mostly what TREES are for, except when the tree is prehensile. ELVES, GNOMES, and WOODSMEN all use them.

**TREES** are unchancy in Fantasyland. There are four kinds:

1. Dwelling places.
   A) As a house built among the branches, in which case you should watch for a rope ladder suddenly descending.
   B) As a domicile inside the trunk of the Tree, in which case the Tree will be very large but the space inside will be larger still, as in a BUILDING.

c) As a space under the roots. Here the dwellers are always hostile and usually DWELL much further underground than you bargained for.

2. Hostile Trees.

    A) Prehensile. These will grab you with their branches and try to eat you.

    B) Mobile. These will quietly move about and get in your way. They may also try to eat you. In extreme cases they will attack BUILDINGS.

    c) Poisonous. Avoid any drips from these.

    D) All these things at once. Run away.

3. Former People. You can tell this kind because their branches make expressive noises and they tend to bleed if you snap a twig off. Tourists please note that meditating in a WOOD can cause *you* to become a Tree too, unless great care is taken. Once a Tree, you are likely to stay that way for quite a while, because Trees live at a slower rate than humans.

4. Supernatural. These are:

    A) A God (See GODDESSES AND GODS). This Tree will be huge and old and in the heart of the WOOD, whence it will control most things that go on in the Wood and often make demands to its worshippers for the SACRIFICE of Tourists.

    B) Inhabited by a Tree spirit. This type is also big and old, and the spirit may not be very friendly, particularly if one of your COMPANIONS carries an AXE. But most such spirits can be bargained with for help when needed. Caution: Do not ask a Tree spirit to go far from its Tree or it and the Tree will both die. Otherwise it will give any help within reason.

    c) An Ash Woman. She will look exactly like a real woman and try to seduce male Tourists lost in a Wood, but

T

if you go round behind her you will find she has no back. She is the shell of a female imprinted on a bent piece of bark. Ash Women can be dangerous. If you find a strange woman in a wood, always go round behind her and check before getting seduced.

 **TRIBES** are what Barbarians have instead of CLANS. Each has a Chieftain and a SHAMAN, and its members (probably) share a surname, such as Jones, or Sons of Thog.

 **TROLLS** are said by some to be a silicon lifeform. They do certainly tend to turn to stone in daylight, however this might happen. They are huge knobbly beings, not very bright, who will attack Tours in moorlands and hilly places. They are also said to live under BRIDGES (when, on the PANCELTIC TOUR, they are often called Kelpies). Formerly you needed only to keep them fighting until sunrise, but nowadays Trolls seem to have become desensitized to daylight and must be destroyed by MAGIC or just driven off, preferably by SWORDS. This is difficult, because they are hugely strong.

 **TROTS, THE.** One of the many nuisances that do not exist in Fantasyland. See ECOLOGY.

 **TROUSERS** are worn by both males and females who are taking part in the action. (N.B.: They are almost never referred to as "pants" or "breeches.") These garments have to be tough, since they are designed to be lived in day and night for some weeks, and so are usually made of leather or thick wool.

See also SMELLS.

**TUNNELS.** The inhabitants of Fantasyland appear to have

T

been, in the recent past, obsessive diggers of Tunnels of all kinds—not only SEWERS. The walls of all large BUILDINGS are *honeycombed*(OMT). Tunnels and UNDERGROUND PASSAGES can be trusted to radiate underground from all CASTLES, CITADELS, CITIES, ISLANDS in lakes, MANSIONS, MONASTERIES, PALACES, and TEMPLES; many RUINS have them too. Nearly all of them at once plunge impractically beneath the nearest RIVER or stretch of WATER and are thus slimy and liable to flooding. Quite a number provide habitats for unspecified slimy critters, and many SMELL. It is hard to see what has prompted this undoubtedly useful obsession with Tunnelling, unless it is an understandable desire to escape from DANGER. One conjecture is that the inhabitants of Fantasyland have not long ago interbred with DWARFS and so find that Tunnelling is in their blood.

A curious thing about the Tunnels in Fantasyland is that, although often the Management has omitted to supply you with any obvious source of LIGHTING, you are almost always able to see where you are going and what you are doing.

**TURNCOATS** are people who change to the side of the DARK LORD in mid-Tour. This can happen to anyone except CHILDREN, GODS, and the TALENTED GIRL. Turncoats are particularly dangerous because they have no *REEK OF WRONGNESS*(OMT). You will have got to know them as a friendly COMPANION, Good KING, Tour MENTOR, etc., and you will trust them with your life/QUEST OBJECT/SECRET without suspecting that they now operate on behalf of EVIL. Such people will have been taken aside during the Tour and been blackmailed, threatened, put to the TORTURE, fed POISON, hypnotised, enchanted by a MAGIC OBJECT, or simply been made an offer they couldn't refuse. After this they will be working very seriously for your downfall. But

T

take heart. The Rule is that only one person becomes a Turn-coat at a time. The Management does not allow everyone in Fantasyland to turn against you at once.

Note that the term Turncoat is never used to describe a person who leaves the cause of the Dark Lord to join yours. This is reasonable. Your side is in the right. People who join you are merely becoming converted.

See also BETRAYAL, MINIONS OF THE DARK LORD, SPIES, and UNPLEASANT STRANGER.

**TYRANTS.** Tyrants are like bad KINGS, only truly atrocious. Most of them seem to rule in the FANATIC CALIPHATES, but they are not unknown among the ARISTOCRATIC FEUDALISTS if things have got out of hand there. They may be REGENTS. Tourists can tell when a COUNTRY is ruled by a Tyrant because the ROAD to the main CITY will be lined with impaled corpses and severed heads will be stuck above the City gates. Expect to be imprisoned and put to the TORTURE here.

T

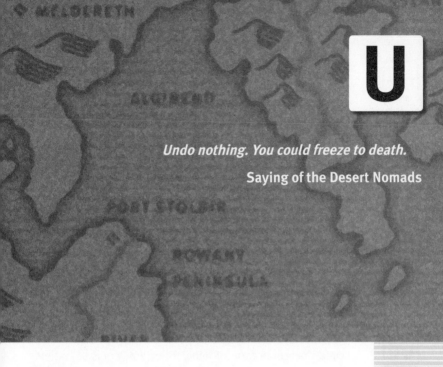

# U

*Undo nothing. You could freeze to death.*

**Saying of the Desert Nomads**

**UNDEAD.** Remarkably few people stay dead when killed in Fantasyland. This may be because it is necessary for a correctly qualified MAGIC USER to SING a person's soul to rest. Without this formality, there is trouble. Even with it, the DARK LORD is likely to come along and raise an ARMY of corpses. The difficulty here is that they cannot be killed a second time, but walk mechanically about minus various limbs, rising up each time they are knocked down, until they are either hacked to pieces or discharged of MAGIC by a MYSTICAL MASTER or Good WIZARD. Expect to encounter at least a squad of Undead from quite early in your Tour. Individual Undead may be met in Barons' MANSIONS, OLD RUINED CITIES, and other desolate places at any time. Unless they have been deliberately summoned by the Tour MENTOR for KNOWLEDGE, they are nothing but bad news. In extreme peril, Tourists too can summon Undead in some numbers, but only on the third leg of the Tour, near the CONCLUSION.

See also NECROMANCY and ZOMBIES.

**UNDERGROUND PASSAGES** are usually there when you need them. No FORT, CASTLE, MONASTERY, or TEMPLE is without one. Thus your escape from an uncomfortable situation or PRISON is assured. Traditionally, the Underground Passage will be down some stone steps from the cellar or DUNGEON, where you may have to clear away some rubble, and then it will be wet and slimy (*dank and dripping* OMT), with puddles underfoot, because it always takes you under the nearest RIVER. It will bring you out a good healthy distance from the DANGER you were escaping, usually into a clump of very prickly undergrowth. This is how the Management takes care of its Tourists.

**UNDERWEAR** is optional and largely nonexistent. It is believed that some form of loincloth or drawers is sometimes permitted, but the Management is naturally coy on this subject. Bras are certainly unknown, but in the case of dancing girls may be replaced by sequined things with tassels.

**UNICORNS** are exceedingly rare. Each one you meet will tell you that it is the last one. Their horns, however, are to be found quite often, and you may use them both for healing and as a magic wand. The rumour that Unicorns still acknowledge VIRGINS is probably false.

**UNPLEASANT STRANGER** is a Tour COMPANION whom no one likes or trusts. Usually the Stranger is male and neither young nor old. He can be either sly and ingratiating or *gruff and taciturn* OMT, and sets everyone's back up and teeth on edge. He will be dressed well but unremarkably. His hair will be dark. This piece of COLOUR CODING often, but not invariably, makes it clear that the Stranger is a SPY for BANDITS or for the DARK LORD, but in his case you have to wait and see. If he is a Spy for Bandits, then you will not have to wait long; if for the Dark Lord, then you have him for most of the Tour. But in some cases he is a dispossessed or long-lost KING, embittered by his past, in which case you will have misjudged him. A fairly sure rule of thumb is to look at the Stranger's hair. If it is greasy, he has to be a Spy. If it is simply *unkempt* <u>OMT</u> or *greying* <u>OMT</u>, or both, he is on the side of GOOD and the Dark Lord is his personal ENEMY; he will be a great help in the Final CONFRONTATION by drawing the Dark Lord's attention to himself while the rest of you work at SAVING THE WORLD.

U
V

*Vengeance is seldom rewarding. You should negotiate payment in advance. The Assassin Huggi forgot this maxim but fortunately did not live to regret it.*

Ka'a Orto'o,
Gnomic Utterances, *V xxiii*

**VALLEYS** are places of importance. They are:

1. The sites of major battles that either take place on the present Tour or took place in the past. If the battle is here and now, the Valley will have been carefully chosen as the site. It will be green and attractive until after the battle, when it will be trampled and *littered with dead and dying* (OMT). If the battle was in the past, the Valley will be a sad place, where *the old agony still clings* (OMT). Sensitive Tourists will find it quite distressing.

2. Hidden and Enchanted, and likely your QUEST OBJECT. Here the Valley will be more than just green. It will be a paradise of wildflowers and stately old TREES. Any WATER will flow melodiously or stand and reflect the view harmoniously. The sky will be azure, the breeze dulcet. The Management really does you proud here. You will feel as if you are home at last. Some of your COMPANIONS may well stay here for good. The rest of you will absorb whatever the ENCHANTMENT has to give you and then

depart, yearning. Later, you will kick yourself for leaving.

**VAMPIRES** are increasingly rare on the Tour. They have been attracted over to the Horror Tour by offers of better pay. Where they appear, you will find up-to-date Vampires wear expensive sunglasses and wish to drain you of energy rather than blood.

**VEGETABLES** are seldom eaten except as a component of STEW. This is odd, because every MARKET has piles of glossy vegetables on display. Raw ones are unknown as part of a meal. The inhabitants insist on everything being cooked, usually for hours, and would certainly faint at the sight of a lettuce. See also ROOTS and SCURVY.

**VESTS.** A sort of V-necked sweater without sleeves, made of leather and usually worn over a SHIRT.

**VESTIGIAL EMPEROR** is nearly always a small, ordinary man (this shows how the VESTIGIAL EMPIRE has shrunk) rattling about in an enormous PALACE. He shows little interest in restoring the former glories of his Empire, but concentrates instead on harmless occupations like botany and gardening. His gardens are always very fine. He will be suave and hospitable to Tourists. But do not underestimate him. That ordinary appearance hides a keen political brain and an up-to-the-minute grasp of local POLITICS. You will find him very proud and snobbish if you chance to want to marry his daughter, but if you want material aid or an ARMY he will tell you at length how pacific and penniless he is. If you work at it, you can marry his daughter and get an Army out of him, but it will take some time and probably an unprovoked attack on the Empire to convince him.

**VESTIGIAL EMPIRE.** The most civilized part of the continent. You can even get decent FOOD and a BATH here. This Empire occupies an area usually slightly larger than most other COUNTRIES and you will know you are in it because the ROADS will be well made and patrolled by Imperial GUARDS in HELMETS and SKIRTS. Rest-houses line the way, a day's march apart. The LANDSCAPE will be full of prosperous farmlands, vineyards, and olive groves, and you may even see a little light INDUSTRY, such as pottery and carpet-making. White villas crown the hills—in fact, most BUILDINGS in the Empire are white. When you reach the imperial City, you will find TEMPLES and colonnades as well as streets of decent houses, drains, and public Baths. The aura of civilization extends to daily life too. The Vestigial Empire is the only Country on the standard Tour to have POLITICS. It has a parliament and a senate and many noble CLANS to jockey for power. This keeps all Imperialists very busy, very noisy, and very likely to POISON one another. They also have time to spare to overcharge most Tourists, since they understand MONEY in a truly civilized way. If you can survive this, you should enjoy the Vestigial Empire. It has a touch of home about it.

**VILLAGES** almost never appear on any MAP, but are quite frequent on most routes; one may even be your STARTING POINT, provided it is sufficiently far from anywhere else. Villages usually consist of one street with houses scattered along it, a lot of barking dogs, a smithy (see BLACKSMITHS), and, if you are lucky, an INN. People who live in Villages tend to be very parochial and suspicious even of GOOD visitors. This is because their life is a constant struggle against poverty and SQUALOR as well as magical drought and other WEATHER. They will have a lot of rather strange beliefs about MAGIC

> **VEGETATION** divides into three kinds: Good, Bad, and Neutral.
> 1. Good is the herbs that always present themselves when you need Healing; the Roots you can find and dig up as soon as your food runs out; and the Waygrass that grows by the road when you have eaten all your Journeybread. On rare occasions, a flower will be a manifestation of a Goddess.
> 2. Bad are all mobile, prehensile, and carnivorous Trees, plants that grow in magical Wastes (**OMT** *of a poisonous green colour*), and the highly toxic thorny bushes that grow where you are trying to push through a Ruin to find a Scroll.
> 3. Neutral are just trees and grass and such, which nobody notices much.

being dangerous and girls needing to wear SKIRTS, but their hearts are in the right place. You will be quite sorry when MUTANT NASTIES emerge from the hinterland and kill them all.

**VIRGINS** are much in demand for various reasons:
1. For SACRIFICE on an ALTAR to a bad God (see GODDESSES AND GODS). The Virgin has to be female, young, good-looking, and wearing white.
2. For WITCHCRAFT. Some schools of WITCHES hold that a Witch retains her POWERS only so long as she is a Virgin. This is probably a myth and causes much unhappiness on most Tours.
3. For sale to a rich person. Most BANDITS and PIRATES go to surprising lengths to ensure their most beautiful young female captives remain Virgins until they are sold as SLAVES. This more than doubles the price they can get.
4. For tempting UNICORNS. The mode of attraction, whereby a Unicorn is brought to lay its head in the lap of a young girl, is probably no longer effective.

U
V

5. For tempting DRAGONS. Again a female Virgin is needed, but this practice is long outmoded.

6. As TALENTED GIRLS. These are very likely, towards the end of the second third of the Tour, to come across a male Tourist in his BATH and turn implausibly to jelly (*a surge of some deep, hitherto unknown emotion swept through her* OMT). Thereafter they have a sprightly step, a jaunty gleam in the eyes, a yet more tiptilted nose, and a private life over which the Management generally draws a discreet veil.

7. Nobody wants a male Virgin at all. Young boys, yes, but there is no stipulation about Virginity. In fact, some experience is preferred.

**VISIONS.** Tourists without TALENT can often be obtuse about how the Management wishes them to act. DREAMS will be tried first. If the unTalented Tourist still refuses to decide to do the right thing, she/he will be accorded a Vision. This will sometimes show the consequences of her/his present reluctance to act, but most often will be a graphic sight of things happening elsewhere which need to be set right at once. Visions can show CITIES burning, ISLANDS sinking, and ARMIES marching, but may also show more domestic scenes in PALACES where the beleaguered young QUEEN is being forced into marriage with her Evil COUNCILLOR. Such sights will galvanize any Tourist. See also PROPHECY.

*When you obtain a talisman of great worth, you should exchange it quickly for a bag of beans. Protection is nothing like as valuable as climbing to the sky.*

**Ka'a Orto'o,
More Gnomic Utterances,** *XXXII xlix*

**WALLED CITIES.** If a City has walls around it, particularly if those walls are spectacularly strong, high, and thick, and if its gates are marvels of sevenfold beaten bronze, then you can BET large odds that it will be under SIEGE before you have been in it three days.

**WANDS** (rare). Another term for STAFFS.

**WAR.** Long ago there was of course the WIZARDS' War, usually accounted the Ultimate Conflict, but War naturally goes on all the time in Fantasyland. It follows the Rules for CONFRONTATIONS, FIGHTS, and INCIDENTS by starting smallish and ending up with the whole continent on a War footing. There is usually dreadful slaughter before the finish. And, like all Wars, this one solves very little. The Tour party has to go in alone and finish the DARK LORD off, either during the main fighting or after it is over. But never fear: GOOD will triumph in the end, though at considerable expense. After the War, there will be a brand-new WASTE AREA ready for the next Tour to visit.

**WAR AND WORSHIP PEOPLE** were once a much larger PEOPLE than they are now. These days they are limited to one remote VALLEY, and some Tours do not even call there. It is easy to see why. Among this People, women spend their days as PRIESTESSES in exclusive service to their GODDESS and occupy any houses there are. Men live apart in Halls and devote their energies to being Warriors. Each sex despises the other. There is some yearly arrangement whereby the sexes can get together for one night. Usually there is a feast at which a potent drink is served. This reduces cultural inhibitions just enough so that the next generation can be conceived. Possibly these days the drink is less potent, or maybe the arrangement is flawed. One serious problem is that neither sex seems to have time either to cultivate fields or to look after children. At any rate, this People is definitely on the decline.

**WARDS** are magical protections. They have to be invoked by a MAGIC USER (usually tired out after a day's travel) who concentrates at four points of a circle, or draws a circle in the earth with a stick, or SINGS. After this, the CAMP will be safe from predators and the forces of EVIL for one night. But do not expect the Magic User to help with the chores afterwards. The Rules state that this form of MAGIC is hard work.

**WARRIOR WOMEN.** The country where these ladies live is almost the only one you will not visit on your Tour. They do not like intruders or men. Rumour has it that there are no men in this country, even for breeding with. Where the next generation comes from or who looks after it is anyone's guess. But the Warrior Women themselves are out and about a lot. They are far more soldierly than male soldiers, and do a lot of swaggering, swearing, screwing, drinking, and betting, as well as fighting. Some are huge and coarse with very hairy armpits, but most are quite slender and comely. They are all naturally very strong. If you want your arm broken, try insulting a Warrior Woman. Nevertheless, it is possible to become quite friendly with them, provided no one treats them like women. Rumour has it that they are all gay. This may be true, but SEX with a Warrior Woman is often provided on a Tour and should not be missed by either men or women.

**WASHING.** Do not expect to wash often. Do not expect warm WATER. Do not expect to wash at all in most INNS. Washing of yourself and clothes will be done mostly in RIVERS and streams. Expect to feel gritty afterwards.

But see also BATH.

**WASTE AREAS** occupy large parts of the main landmass. Each has a different origin:

1. A KING's personality defects. Here the land reflects the King and parches dry or simply refuses to grow crops. The inhabitants are forced to leave. This Waste is full of derelict farms and often has very unreliable WEATHER.
2. Overtaxation. Here the LANDSCAPE looks like the first kind, but seems quite lush. The peasantry have all sold up because they were unable to pay the extortionate taxes demanded by their Lord.
3. A recent visit by the DARK LORD or his ARMIES. Ashes and corpses are left in their wake. Again, land and farms are empty, though there may be a few pitiful survivors to tell you what happened (see NUNNERY).

4. One-time lands of the VESTIGIAL EMPIRE. As the Empire shrank, the lands were simply left empty. Before that they must have been perilously over-cropped. All that is left now are miles of tussocky grass, broken ROADS, and stumps of BUILDINGS overgrown with bushes and weeds. There are almost no BIRDS or ANIMALS here; MUTANT NASTIES, WERES, and MONSTERS have usually moved in. Tours need to go warily in this Waste.

5. Remains of the WIZARDS' WAR. Go even more warily here. This Waste is still full of magical pollution. There are areas of glassy slag and creeping MIST. The vegetation is weird and often a strident green. It will eat you. Twisted TREES, in particular, are quite clever at acquiring human prey. Slimes and mosses will try to absorb your flesh. Thorns will poison you. Rocks are likely to try to kill you. And any Animal seen will be frightfully mutated into something in-telligent, vile, and predatory.

**WATER.** You may drink from or wash in any Water, however scummy, while on the Tour, except in the MARSHES, where it is full of wriggly things. Water in Fantasyland does not harbour germs. The only other Water it is unwise to touch will be either near the home of an ENCHANTRESS or on the trail left by a WIZARD. This may turn you into things or show you disturbing pictures.

But see BATH and SEX.

**WATERBOTTLES.** Heavy leather bags for taking water along in on a JOURNEY. They customarily hang by the saddle. Most of them have slow punctures. They always prove to be emptier than you thought, and invariably prove to be quite empty a day or two after you started crossing a desert.

**WATERFALLS** are generally very tall and thin (see LAND-SCAPE). If the Management draws your attention to a Waterfall, it will not be for its scenic value. It will be because there are CAVES or a hiding place or a secret colony of friendly folk behind it. You will have to turn sideways and slither along the rock to reach it.

**WAYBREAD OR JOURNEY CAKE** is a flat cake, infinitely nutritious and weighing almost nothing, on which Tourists may sustain themselves for long periods. In appearance, it seems to be halfway between a ricecake and a ship's biscuit, and in substance, it is truly remarkable since those eating it are never hungry and absolutely never suffer from any deficiency disease (see SCURVY). In some areas there is also a kind of grass capable of being eaten instead of Waybread, but this seems to grow only when your Waybread has run out. It is strange that the inhabitants, given the remarkable properties of Waybread and grass, do not choose to live entirely on one or the other. The reason must be that neither tastes of anything very much. After a month of eating them you will even be glad of STEW.

**WEAPONMASTER.** The ex-GLADIATOR or MERCENARY who runs the SCHOOL OF WEAPONRY. The Rules state that he will be in late middle age but extremely fit, with iron-grey hair, broad shoulders, and a scar somewhere on his face. In his day he has been a legend. Nor has he lost any of his skills. So good is he that he will seldom take on any of his pupils unless they show extreme promise. He leaves tuition to helpers and sparring partners, so how he keeps himself fit is a bit of a mystery. He may look forbidding, but this is just to hide his nice nature. When you have been in his School long enough to show promise, you will become his friend. He will give you tips that are invaluable in the arena. You will try to persuade him to come with you on the Tour, but you will seldom succeed. If you do, though, he will be a valuable COMPANION.

**WEAPONS.** Essentially, see AXE, BOWS AND ARROWS, DAGGER, GUNS, and SWORDS. In addition, spears, pikes, and halberds may be used by militias, tridents by GLADIATORS, and scythes and cudgels by AVERAGE FOLK. A few exotic Weapons, such as throwing stars, are sometimes permitted to FEMALE MERCENARIES. The GAY MAGE may use a crossbow, but otherwise crossbows are reserved for bad people. Magical Weapons were banned after the WIZARDS' War, but may still be in evidence—their use is a sure sign that the wielder is EVIL.

**WEATHER** is always wrong for what you are doing at the time. It varies from heat/drought if you must travel quickly, to heavy rain if you need just to travel. If you need to sleep rough, there is always a frost; invariably, if you have to cross MOUNTAINS, there will be a thunderstorm or blizzard. Some of the reason for this is that, despite obvious drawbacks, the Management nearly always arranges for Tours to set out in late autumn or early winter (see SEASONS). The rest is natural perversity. Weather is, too, remarkably apt to reflect the emotions of the Tour party. It is sullen and grey if the party is quarrelling among itself, bright and springlike if everyone is happy. It is also very susceptible to MAGIC, particularly at sea, where STORMS can be raised in instants (see STORM CONTROL), and in DESERTS, where dust storms can be created almost as quickly. The general advice here is to keep smiling and avoid annoying WIZARDS.

**WERES.** These are people who change from human to ANI-MAL form either at will or involuntarily under the full MOON (see SHAPESHIFTING). Few can take more than one sort of Animal form, but the Animals chosen are various. There are reports that a Were beagle has been sighted. Not all Weres are unfriendly to Tourists, but most are.

See also WEREWOLVES.

**WEREWOLVES** and other WERES still prowl the WASTE AREAS, but in decreasing numbers. Most of them have gone over to the Horror Tour in search of better working conditions and more prey. However, the sight of an apparent woman or man suddenly shortening in the body, elongating in the face, and then dropping to all fours while she/he grows a lot of rank grey hair is still a great Tourist attraction and should not be missed. But have your silver weapon ready. A Were will spring before the change is complete. You should not let her/him take you by surprise.

See also SHAPESHIFTING and WOLVES.

**WHARF.** The OMT here is *scummy* and refers to both the wood or stone surface of the Wharf and the water beside it. Wharfs are full of picturesque SQUALOR.

See also BALES, BOATS, FISH, SHIPS, and THIEVES' GUILD.

**WILD HUNT.** This crosses the paths of Tourists scarily at un-predictable intervals, often through the sky and nearly always at night. It is very *numinous* (OMT) and also *doom-laden* (OMT). Otherwise no one knows quite what to make of it. Normally all that can be distinguished of it is the barking of many hounds, the galloping of many HORSES, and the one rider, horned and masked, at its head. Possibly none of it is fully within the control of the Management, since its appearances often occur arbitrarily, and perfectly well-conducted Tourists who witness it tend thereafter to become *numinous* and *doom-laden* themselves.

**WINE** is always served in tankards like BEER (and may well foam in the same way). It is traditionally kept in leather containers. No one knows why bottles are not used. Glass exists. Most windows are glazed. But the inhabitants seem to prefer wine tasting of ANIMAL SKIN.

**WISE OLD STRANGER.** Usually a MAGIC USER and possibly your Tour MENTOR. In neither case should a Tourist be rude to him, though he will often be extremely irritating. If he is not your Mentor, his MAGIC will not be so powerful and his personality may well be timid, but it is still inadvisable to cross him; he will anyway die desperately trying to save you and your COMPANIONS during a magical attack. You just have to be patient. If, however, this person is female, you are stuck with her. She may be old as the hills, but she is also tough as old boots and could well outlive everyone else on the Tour. And she is so Wise you want to hit her.

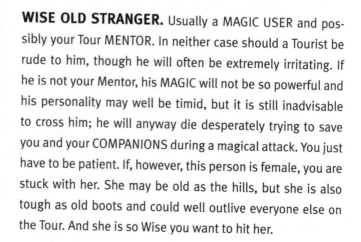

**WITCHCRAFT** is the Herbal and more personal end of MAGIC. It can be either EVIL or GOOD.
See also HERBS, HERBWOMAN, and WITCHES.

**WITCHES** are special and probably at least the equal of WIZARDS. They come in several kinds:
1. GOOD. These are the commonest type. Most of them seem to be, at most, in their early thirties, and they are often good-looking and extremely well dressed. All of them have commanding personalities and great skill in MAGIC, but from time to time they show an endearing

lack of confidence in themselves. This is because they are alienated from normal society. Witches of this type normally live in a College or Hall sited in a remote spot, along with numerous other Witches and governed by strict Rules and an even stricter Mother Superior. This establishment will have sent the Witch forth with instructions to perform a task, such as SAVING THE WORLD, that she feels to be almost beyond her power. You may become quite friendly with this type of Witch, but do not attempt to have SEX with her unless she invites you. A condition of her POWERS may be that she remains a VIRGIN. But you never know.

2. Bad. (See ENCHANTRESS, which is really the same thing.) This kind seems younger than Good Witches, but it is not the case. They always prolong their life, looks, and youth indefinitely by their arts.

3. Freelance. These are rarer and tend to be:
   A) Mature ladies who have decided to strike out on their own, in which case they look like bad Witches or are fat, overdressed, and silly-seeming. In very rare cases they may be retiring and ugly. They live in CITIES and can usually be persuaded to join your cause.
   B) A very young Witch in search of more Magic or adventure, who will probably join the Tour. You may not realize she is a Witch until there is a magical attack of some kind (see INCIDENT) and she is forced to help. Then she counts as a COMPANION.

**WITCHFIRE** is the insubstantial burning substance which MAGIC USERS can cast at ENEMIES. It also appears at sea during STORMS. This makes it clear that the phenomenon is akin, at least, to St. Elmo's Fire.

Compare MAGELIGHT and WITCHLIGHT.

W
X
Y
Z

**WITCHLIGHT.** Really just another word for MAGELIGHT or WITCHFIRE. In the case of Witches, this light can flame from the hair and surround the hands. Some manifestations of MAGIC are clearly sex-linked.

 **WITCH SIGHT** is the ability to see through ILLUSIONS and to spot Magical events, invisible persons, ELVES, and the nimbus surrounding a Spellworking. It is a truly useful GIFT. All MAGIC USERS seem to have it. In some cases it entails the ability to see patterns that others cannot perceive. Tourists without it must regard themselves as seriously disabled.

  **WIZARDS** are normally intensely old. They live solitary lives, mostly in TOWERS or CITADELS, or in a special CITY which has facilities for study. They will have been studying MAGIC for centuries and, alas, the great majority have been seriously dehumanized by those studies. Two-thirds have become EVIL, possibly agents of the DARK LORD. The remaining GOOD one-third have become eccentrics or drunks or just very hard to understand. Evil or Good, Wizards are the strongest MAGIC USERS of all except for the DARK LORD and GODDESSES AND GODS, and can usually be distinguished by the fact that they have long beards and wear ROBES.

You need to distinguish Wizards: if crossed, most Wizards get childishly offended and exact terrible revenge. Angry Wizards are likely to throw lumps of LANDSCAPE hither and thither, move MOUNTAINS, wave WEATHER systems about (see STORM CONTROL), hurl DEMONS, flood or bury CITIES, and pollute whole COUNTRIES with sleeting Magics. This is how the WIZARDS' WAR seems to have come about: too many Wizards got too annoyed at once.

As a result, full-scale Magic Wars have been prohibited

## HOW TO INTERACT WITH WIZARDS

Treat all Wizards with the utmost politeness, even if one of them is your Tour MENTOR and you are trying to bully her/him into providing some action or telling you something. Remember that Wizards do not need anything from you and do not like to be coerced. Even the smiling ones with bushy eyebrows are touchy on this point.

Evil Wizards are liable to immure you in ice, bury you alive, or just transmit you to the Breeding Pens as food for their MONSTERS. Be highly civil.

Good Wizards do not go so far. They will just remove your skin and then make you itch. Be *very* courteous.

Poor Wizards, who are bad at MAGIC, need to be treated with even greater politeness, unctuously in fact. If they botch the SPELL they put on you in anger, they might turn you into *anything* and then not be able to undo it. Positively crawl to these.

And, please, please, *never* attempt to seduce a female Wizard. The consequences can be terrible.

by the Rules. Nowadays most Wizards are bored. Evil ones have to occupy their time with BREEDING PROGRAMMES and plans to reign over the world. Good Wizards could not do this, and so the Tours have come as a godsend to them. Some Good Wizards can accompany the Tourists as MENTORS, and all of them have fun bossing the show and delivering PROPHECIES or cryptic advice. And the Management in its turn is grateful to the Wizards, both for making the Tours so interesting and for obligingly putting all the Landscape back together again after each Final CONFRONTATION, so that the next Tour may visit Fantasyland and find it whole and entire, as if as always.

See also APPRENTICES and HEDGE WIZARD.

**WOLVES** can sometimes be heard howling in the winter wastes, but are not actually present. No Wolf has ever attacked a Tour party. If you see a Wolf, it will be either a normal WERE or one of the shapes your Tour MENTOR can assume at will. The colour of its eyes will tell you if it is friendly or not. WEREWOLVES in Fantasyland tend to be red-eyed. A WIZARD or other MAGIC USER will, in Wolf shape, either retain her/his normal eye colour or have silver eyes.

See also COLOUR CODING and SHAPESHIFTING.

**WOODS** are frequent, and some of them are just Woods where you CAMP. Others are different. You can tell which because, from the moment you enter the other type of Wood you will have *a sense of being watched*(OMT). There are two basic kinds:

1. There are Dwellers, human or Other, who are up TREES watching you. Expect an arrow here that will just miss you and stick in either a tree trunk or a FELLOW TRAVELLER who has not been allotted a NAME. This will be followed either by ladders descending from above or by the Dwellers themselves, unheard and unseen, surrounding the Tour party and preventing escape.

2. The Wood is a sentient entity—ground, vegetation, ANIMALS, and all. Here the Wood is watching you. It will shortly herd you by vegetable means inwards to its very heart, where there will be a mound or a Tree. You have to get into communication with this type of Wood as soon as possible, or it will get angry and either attack you or just make sure you fail to get out and starve to death. When you do succeed in talking to it, you will gain profound wisdom from it. Woods are one of the few places where SELF-KNOWLEDGE is often acquired, but

you usually have to earn this by having a bad time first. See also FOREST OF DOOM.

**WOODSMEN** live in the WOODS and can be either human or Other. They seldom join a Tour, but are often met in the course of it. Frequently they are hostile and suspicious to begin with. You may have to work hard to get them on the side of the Tour. Mostly they simply want to go on living privately. This is particularly true if they are nymphs or satyrs, who are the only kind of Woods people to DWELL on the ground. All other types live up TREES and come down on long rope ladders to parley. Most of them are wonderful trackers and make very useful scouts in the ARMY of the GOOD. The majority also have trained BIRDS, which are telepathically bonded to their owners—this makes the Woodsmen's scouting even more effective. Quite a few Woodsmen are also MAGIC USERS, often of a strange and powerful kind, having imbibed the *secrets of Nature* OMT from the Woods over the centuries. Tourists are advised to be very polite to Woodsmen, however extraordinary they might look.

Many human Woodsmen have mutated into skinny, silver-haired Elflike beings, but should never be mistaken for ELVES. Elves would object. They live in Woods up Trees too, and wish to remain distinct.

**WORK** is seldom done as such in Fantasyland. When it is inevitable, it is always known as Toil. But few *dwellers* OMT — with the notable exception of INNKEEPERS, HEALERS, and the occasional FERRYMAN — actually have anything like a job or gainful employment. They just sort of live. And it is a Rule that no member of the Tour party has a job of any kind. They are all, in various ways, out of Work.

*Xerostomia, otherwise extreme dryness of the mouth, has many causes but only one cure: the nearest inn.*

*Ka'a Orto'o,*
**Gnomic Utterances, I i**

**XENOPHOBIA** is displayed by most of the PEOPLES of Fantasyland. If they have a supernumerary appendage, as they quite often do, you will be treated as a freak for having only the requisite two of whatever it is. However, they are unlikely to SACRIFICE you for this small fault; more likely they will befriend you in a patronizing fashion and thereafter make sly digs about the fact that you are inferior. Which, you will deduce halfway through the second brochure, you probably are: where can you store your JEWELS without that second navel?

If the Peoples have the usual number of appendages, they normally express their xenophobia by enslaving you.

*Yield gracefully when someone pushes in front of you. You can then stab them in the back.*

Ka'a Orto'o,
Gnomic Utterances, *X xx*

**YEAR KING.** Rarely seen on the Tour these days, the Year King rules for but a year before being made the subject of a hideous SACRIFICE. Nevertheless, there are lots of volunteers for the post, possibly because of the positive effect a lusty Year King can have on the LANDSCAPE and even the COUNTRY as a whole, possibly because of all the fun he is allowed to have creating that positive effect.

**YOGURT.** The health-conscious Tourist's alternative to STEW. Yogurt is served on the one occasion when you are ravenously hungry and would *murder* for a nice filling bowl of Stew. Nevertheless, you smile politely and make appreciative noises, because the person serving it to you is an attractive member of the opposite sex and, after the meal (if such it can be called), you plan to take a BATH.

**ZODIAC.** The constellations of Fantasyland are quite different from those we see in our own skies. Nevertheless, ASTROLOGY follows a very similar system. Expect Doom when the Angry Red Planet is in the Eye of the Shovel. Do not be frightened if the Morning Star is widdershins to the Rabbit, because this is likely a sign of Good Fortune. The Management is allowed to make such stuff up as it goes along until the sky is positively crowded out with improbable constellations and multiple conjunctions. The MOON, often full or *gibbous*(OMT) for months on end, will play a large part in all this.

**ZOMBIES.** These are just the UNDEAD, except nastier, more pitiable, and generally easier to kill. When you slash your SWORD across their stomachs—which you will inevitably do—they watch their impossibly decayed intestines pour out in a glob, and then look at you with *an expression of ultimate pathos*(OMT) before crumpling at the knees. Naturally they SMELL quite strongly.

**DIANA WYNNE JONES** was born in London, England. At the age of eight, she suddenly knew she was going to be a writer, although she was too dyslexic to start until she reached age twelve. There were very few books for children in the house, so Diana wrote stories for herself and her two younger sisters. She received her B.A. at St. Anne's College in Oxford before she began to write full-time.

Her many remarkable novels include the award-winning *Archer's Goon*, *Howl's Moving Castle* (made into a major animated feature by Japanese director Hayao Miyazaki), *Fire and Hemlock*, the Dalemark Quartet, *Dark Lord of Derkholm* (which arose from the writing of *The Tough Guide to Fantasyland*), *Year of the Griffin*, *The Merlin Conspiracy*, and the Chrestomanci books (*Charmed Life, Witch Week, The Lives of Christopher Chant, The Magicians of Caprona, Conrad's Fate,* and her most recent novel, *The Pinhoe Egg*).

Diana Wynne Jones lives with her husband, the medievalist J. A. Burrow, in Bristol, England, the setting of many of her books. They have three grown sons and five grandchildren.

Her Web site is **www.leemac.freeserve.co.uk**

# HOW I CAME TO WRITE THIS GUIDEBOOK

Late in 1994, I was recovering from surgery, a situation I found myself in rather often during that decade. This time I was more than usually bored and impatient. Knowing this, John Clute suggested that I might help Chris Bell work through the projected entries for *The Encyclopedia of Fantasy*, which he was then compiling with John Grant. It was the perfect occupation. I lay in bed. Chris arrived every morning with an enormous sheaf of printouts (for there were many more proposed entries than actually appeared in the finished *Encyclopedia*) and we both got to work. Our job was to decide whether each entry was necessary, to suggest new ones, to discuss whether some of the entries made sense (many didn't), and to provide examples in support of what each entry said.

Well, we had after a week or so reached the letter *N* and the entry for *Nunnery* when I realised that we had for most of the time been speaking in chorus, we knew most of the books concerned so well. Then, we said in unison, "Nunneries are for sacking! There is usually one survivor." And both burst out laughing. I said, "You know, most of these books are so much the same that I could write the guidebook for the country they happen in." Chris said, "Yes, but we're on *O* now. Do they really need this entry called *Obsessed Seeker*?" I forget what I answered. I was too busy realising that I could and should write the guidebook to Fantasyland.

I started *The Tough Guide* a few days later and became so immersed in it that I am, to this day, a little vague about the later parts of the *Encyclopedia*, and almost forgot to do my own entry for it, on *Magic*. John Grant, for a very patient man, became almost impatient with me. But I think he forgave me when he was asked to be copy editor of the first edition of *The Tough Guide to Fantasyland*. He enjoyed it so much that he kept ringing me up and suggesting further entries, and he added quite a few new jokes.

— **Diana Wynne Jones**
Autumn 2006

— **NOTES** —